Let a Smile Be Your Umbrella

Let a Smile Be Your Umbrella

BUT DON'T GET A MOUTHFUL OF RAIN

by JOEY REYNOLDS

HATHERLEIGH PRESS

New York

791.44
Rey

Red Brick Press
An Independent Imprint of Hatherleigh Press

Copyright © 2000 by Joey Reynolds

Red Brick Press
An Independent Imprint of Hatherleigh Press
An Affiliate of W.W. Norton & Company, Inc.
5-22 46th Avenue, Suite 200
Long Island City, NY 11101
1-800-367-2550

Printed in Canada

This edition is printed on acid-free paper that meets the American
National Standards Institute z39-48 Standard.

Library of Congress Cataloging-in-Publication Data
Reynolds, Joey
Let a smile be your umbrella, but don't get a
mouthful of rain / by Joey Reynolds.
p. cm.
ISBN 1-57826-036-1 (alk. paper)
1. Reynolds, Joey. 2. Radio broadcasters--United
States--Biography.
I. Title.
PN1991.4.R439 A3 2000
791.44 028 092--dc21   99-088439
[B]   CIP

All Red Brick Press titles are available for bulk purchase,
special promotions, and premiums. For more information,
please contact the manager of our Special Sales Department
at 1-800-367-2550.

Designed by DC Design

10 9 8 7 6 5 4 3 2 1

Dedicated
to the memory of
Tom Shovan,
radio's unsung hero—and mine

Work as if you don't need the money,
Love as if you've never been hurt, and
Dance as if nobody's watching.

Contents

Preface

As the old spiritual goes, I once was lost but now am found—and I've got a lot of people to thank for finding me.

First of all, it's good to be found at WOR (that's 710 on your AM dial in New York City). Since its inception, WOR has been continuously broadcasting the same format—talk radio—and doing so longer than any other station in America. I've come to believe that WOR stands for World's Oldest Radio.

I'm particularly grateful to David Bernstein, WOR's program director, who had the good sense and gumption to hire me when one of his bosses, general manager Bob Bruno, was out sick and the other, Buckley Broadcasting president Rick Buckley, was away on vacation. Since I had worked for Rick twice before (he fired me the first time; I quit the second), I'm also grateful to him for not kicking me back out on my butt as soon as he saw me behind the mic. (You know what they say, Rick—third time's a charm....) David helped to persuade him that I'd not only keep the ears of our older listeners, but bring in some younger listeners, too.

I'd also like to thank some good friends who've kept me going through the years: Claude Hall, former editor of *Billboard* and foremost friend and confidant; Bob Crewe, who with the Four Seasons created my jingle; Seymour Stein and Ron Alexenberg, who fed my career and my ego till I weighed well over 300 pounds; Wally Clark and Jeff Rich, the guys at *Radio Today* who perked up many of my yesterdays; Barry Bergman, music promoter, publisher, and pal;

Gertie Hossman, who helped me buy my first car
when I was in Ashland, Ohio; Hartford station
manager Charlie Parker, who gave me permission
to be successful; John Pasco, my roommate at
NYU; John Antoon, whose friendship made
sobering up a little less dry; Dick Robinson, head
of the Connecticut School of Broadcasting, who
has always been there to teach me a thing or two;
Russ Oasis, who has made stations bloom in
broadcasting's barrens; Dr. James Chenitz, who
helped my wife and me after I lost my job at
WNBC; Lou Yager, who put me back on track
after a high-speed derailment; Geoff DeVaul,
who helped me cook up my cheesecake company;
Eileen, the Cheesecake Queen; David Fisher and
Rosemary Gannascoli, who make sales bloom at
Bloomie's; Elena, my first producer at WOR;
Kenny Kramer, the "original" Kramer, who
makes reality more fun to tour; Myra Chanin,
Mother Wonderful and a wonderful guest;
Bickram Choudhury, the yoga master who keeps
me limber; Joyce Keller, psychic and sidekick;
Mickey Freeman, stand-up comic and stand-up
friend; Sid Bernstein, the legendary music pro-

moter who brought both The Beatles to Carnegie
Hall and the art of fine dining to my table;
Robert Fleisher, artist, friend, and photographer
who has chronicled my career in pictures ; Art
Vuolo, who has chronicled my career on tape—as
well as the careers of many broadcasting giants;
and, speaking of broadcasting giants, Soupy
Sales, friend and mentor.

My gratitude also goes out to Les Paul, whose
vision and inventions have helped shape 20th century music. About three years ago, I got on the air
and read a bit of misinformation: "Did ya hear?" I
said. "Les Paul died!" Ten minutes later, I got a
call from the deceased. He set me straight and
then wanted to know who the hell I was. I told
him I was a renowned DJ. He said he'd never
heard of me.

As if to prove my obscurity, he brought a
bunch of volumes of *Who's Who in Radio and
Broadcasting* down to my station. He dumped
them on my desk and said, "You're not in any of
these! *You're* the one who doesn't exist!" He stood
there, awaiting an explanation for why I wasn't in
those books.

"'Cause I never took payola," I said. Ever since, Les and I have been buddies. See Les, I finally figured out how to get my name in a book.

Last, I'd like to thank my editor, Heather Ogilvie, who diverted my stream of consciousness into little pools of prose.

Joey Reynolds
December 1999

Let a Smile Be Your Umbrella

CHAPTER 1

Show Biz Kid

Joey was always a little ahead of his mind.

—Father Timothy, O. F. M.,
my ninth grade teacher at Bishop Timon High School

They say that people who get into show business lack self-esteem or come from a dysfunctional environment (not me—I'm from Buffalo). Nowadays we use all these convenient buzzwords to explain ourselves. We assume that anyone who wants to be in show business must have something wrong with him. Want to be a lawyer? A schoolteacher? President of the United States? Well, then, there must be something wrong with you, too.

We analyze ourselves to find excuses, to find people to blame. We never seem to analyze ourselves to find the *good*. Instead of looking for people to blame for who we are, we should *celebrate* who we are and what makes us unique. Even a guy like me—who's been addicted to drugs and alcohol, fired more times than I can count, divorced, humiliated, and cheated—can find reason to celebrate. I've tried to learn from my mistakes and misfortunes. I realize that without them, I wouldn't have been able to experience the joys and wonders of life. And there have been plenty of those.

So despite what pop psychologists would have you believe, each person in show business comes from a different place, has a different goal, and takes a different journey. We're all just trying to fulfill the saying, "to thine own self be true." I was lucky—I learned that saying early. But it took me a little longer to realize that I could be true to others at the same time. . . .

As a kid I realized that I was different. I was always very Hollywood, which is not a good thing to be when you're in Buffalo. Although it's not quite as bad as being in Hollywood and going very Buffalo.

The people in Buffalo are average folks. They get up every morning and have corn flakes. They read the obits to see if they're still there.

My family lived in a poor neighborhood. My mother came to America from Italy, and my father was a fighter. A middleweight, he was a Golden Gloves champ before I was born. He was very strong and handsome and rugged, and he made my mother swoon.

After they got married, my dad went to work as a laborer in the steel plant. My grandfather was in management there. One time the laborers, including my father, went on strike. My grandfather and my father didn't speak for 14 years because of it. It was a ridiculous family feud because it was about business, not family. But in the Forties, Republic Steel *was* the community; it *was* Buffalo.

So my father became bitter about my grandfather, and my grandfather became bitter about my dad. We lived three doors away from Grandpa and we kids were not allowed to speak to him—and he wasn't particularly warm and friendly with us. All I remember about him was that he used to send me out to a tree to get a twig, and then he would whittle it down and spank me on the ass with it. That was his idea of being affectionate.

Over the years, my dad made his living as a steelworker, a taxi driver, and eventually he owned a restaurant and a junkyard. He drank beer and played cards. He was an average Joe, and my mom was a housewife.

Completing the family portrait were my two sisters. Naturally, I felt they were always treated better than I was. With my mom and my sisters, the females outnumbered the males in my family. (Now that I have two daughters, they still do.)

Despite sibling rivalries, my older sister Anna was my hero. She protected and defended me. She used to beat up the neighborhood kids when they picked on me. We were the last white family in a black neighborhood, and I was always at the center of attention. The kids on the block would tease me and I'd fire back with wise-ass remarks, and then the fists would fly. That's when my sister would come to the rescue. She was the fighter Dad wanted *me* to be.

When I was 12, I found out by accident that Anna was my dad's stepchild. She was my mother's daughter from an earlier marriage, which I knew nothing about—until one day when I went poking around in my mom's cedar chest and saw the papers. I was devastated. Numb. I wanted to deny it. I never said anything to my mother. I asked my sister about it, but she pretended it wasn't true. Then she was protecting me in a different sort of way.

Time was, family members would protect each other from any sort of "impropriety," which is what divorce was considered back then. In those days kids were under the witness protection program. Parents "protected" their kids out of kindness, but it could be a mistaken kindness. Now, of course, there are no family secrets. Sometimes, that's a good thing. Putting things in the light and discussing them leads to greater love and understanding. But too often today, by telling our kids everything, we probably tell them too much—and we do it on Jerry Springer.

Dad used to drag me to all the fights, which I wasn't interested in. I hated watching people beat each other up—I saw enough of that in our own neighborhood. But he always wanted me to be in fights. The way I see it, whenever you push somebody in one direction, he's going to pull in another.

But more than trying to push me toward becoming an athlete, my parents tried to pull me *away* from being in show business. They didn't want me to be in show business in any way, shape, or form. That, of course, was all the encouragement I needed.

EAT AT JOEY'S

After he worked at the steel plant, my father owned a restaurant. It was called Joe's Diner. How clever. It was a little greasy spoon that served regular working folks. Since my dad was a former boxer, sports people would come in and drink coffee and talk to him about all the fights and the day's games. And my relatives would come over and play cards during the slow time between lunch and dinner. The fare wasn't fancy, but my dad made great turkey and other roasts.

Naturally, my father made the turkey for Thanksgiving every year. He was diligent about it. He would stand over the bird, basting it religiously every ten minutes for hours. In those days you had to cook a turkey for 10 hours. We didn't use aluminum foil back then, either—we put it in a *paper bag*. Now things have changed—you just throw the bird in plastic and wait till that thing pops out.

The restaurant was time consuming, and I came to hate it because it took my parents away from me. It seemed they were never around. I had a lot of time on my hands at home so I would play around in the kitchen. My mother used to call me "Chef Pierre" and "the mad scientist" because I was always experimenting. She'd come home to find that I always had some kind of food on the ceiling.

I would experiment with whatever there was in the kitchen—that's how I came to make the cheesecake I sell through Bloomingdale's and the Home Shopping Channel. I was trying to make a key lime pie, but there wasn't any condensed milk. So I wound up making a key lime cheesecake because we had cream cheese. I was fearless.

When I was growing up, we made no connection between diet and health. Of course, all that's changed now. One of my daughters is a vegetarian, and I respect that. So last week when I made a turkey for everybody, I also made a vegetarian lasagna for her. I used all organic vegetables and tofu, which takes on the taste of anything it's next to. (So don't put it too close to your mother-in-law.)

I got even more "encouragement" from the priests at Bishop Timon High School. The priests gave me a hard time because I wasn't disciplined. The Church was (and still is) very narrow and rigid, though a lot of kids find comfort in the discipline. Not me. I didn't like algebra, and I didn't like Latin. I always wanted to create and stretch—you know, be true to myself. It wasn't just to be outrageous or to get attention. I wanted to express myself a little, do some things my way. And, of course, that created a conflict.

I wasn't exactly the class clown, though. The class clown was a headliner—I was only a warm-up act. But I had a very active imagination and was always trying to create a scene.

And bright ideas were always coming to me. Like the time I opened an amusement park in my backyard. I dug holes and pushed kids around in wheelbarrows. It didn't take much to entertain kids back before Barney and video games.

The park was successful, so I took it one step farther. I built tents, showed movies in my garage, and charged admission to get in. And then I was on to something.

When I was given a 16mm sound projector for Christmas one year, I began renting films like *Frankenstein* and Abbott and Costello movies and charged kids in the neighborhood to come see them. I got in trouble for it because parents didn't like me to charge their kids. I was entrepreneurial, but I wasn't a good businessman. A good businessman would make the money and not care who got upset.

I guess you could say I expanded too quickly when I made a deal with the priest to use the church hall to show movies. It drew too many people—it was bigger than bingo. The priest wasn't real happy about that. (Nobody messes with bingo.)

He was doing me a favor, letting me have a little fun, but he didn't realize it was going to be a big neighborhood event. Plus, I wasn't very good with the projector, so the priest had to change the reels. I was more the idea man. (I guess things haven't changed much.) So that night I learned that if you are going to draw a big crowd in a borrowed church hall, someone had better yell "Bingo!" every 15 minutes or so just to keep the tension down.

I hounded my parents to let me quit Catholic school and go to public school so I could learn a trade. I wanted to be a projectionist or be involved in the movie business in some other way. They kept fighting me, and finally I failed my freshman year at Bishop Timon High School. After a big struggle, they had to let me quit because I wasn't getting along.

I went to public school, where I lasted a week. The grade I went into was about a year behind my Catholic school in academic studies. Even though I flunked the same studies at Catholic school, flunking the second time around just made me impatient and frustrated. I thought I knew what I wanted to do, but all I really knew was that I wasn't learning it there. At first, I thought I wanted to be a projectionist, but then I decided I really wanted to own the theater. And then I didn't want to own the theater; I wanted to make movies. And then I didn't really want to make movies; I wanted to have some sort of marketing input. But I didn't know how to say that because marketing wasn't a subject they taught in high school.

It wasn't all so tough. Life for a kid back then was 35 cents a day: It was 10 cents for a Coke and a quarter for cigarettes. It was going to drive-in movies with the gang and dancing in the basement to rock 'n' roll. The school's record hops were really popular, too—one night, the school got Jerry Lee Lewis to perform. Actually, it was a local disc jockey who brought Lewis to our Friday night dance—for an extra fee, of course. Back in those days, the school would get 10 percent of the action, and the disc jockey would get 90. (These days it's just the opposite.) For a dollar a head, the DJ could pull in 600 screaming boys (plus the girls from Mount Mercy High School, who were allowed to come over on Fridays to dance with us). The school got its 10 percent, the DJ got his 90, and Jerry Lee Lewis did the appearance just to have his records played. Back then, DJs had a lot of clout.

But between school and life in our neighborhood, I still wanted more.

So for another outlet, I joined the Boys Club in the neighborhood, which is what poor kids did. We had Friday night dances, too, and I used to play the records there. That meant I got attention. I performed a service and started to feel good about myself. I was gaining the respect of my friends because I was doing a job they appreciated.

One day in 1956, a few friends and I took over the PA system, otherwise known as WBCB, of the Buffalo Boys Club. We broadcast news and music shows from 3:00 to 9:00pm. I suppose that was my first official stint as a disc jockey.

A few years later, I went on TV, WGR Channel 2, on a Saturday dance party show. It was a precursor to *American Bandstand*—every city had one. Buddy Deane was the host in Baltimore, Carl Race was in Pittsburgh, and New York had Clay Cole.

My job was to do teen news. And during the music, I got to dance in the background. I remember dancing with a black girl on television, which embarrassed my father because white boys didn't do that back then.

The main attraction, the guy who got to dance front and center, was Mickey DeFiglia. That was not considered a good show business name. He went to Bennett High School, so he started calling himself Michael Bennett, after the school. You've probably heard of him. He went on to choreograph *A Chorus Line* and *Dream Girls* and a bunch of other Broadway shows. Well, he was already choreographing when he was 13. He used to dance with two girls on the show. They used to squabble all the time; he kept pushing them out of the way to get more camera space. But he was a great talent. He could dance like no one I'd ever seen—you couldn't imagine anybody dancing that way.

It was when I was working Saturdays at the TV station that I got a pretty big break. (Or at least, I thought it'd be.) Bill Mazer, the local sportscaster, held a contest for the Announcer of the Future. (Bill went on to become a national sportscaster on TV and radio.) Since I wasn't considered an employee of the station, I was able to enter the contest, which was sponsored by a car company. Each of the contestants aired an announcement, and teenagers signed the petitions of the "announcer" they liked best. I entered the contest and I won it. They gave me some money and a spot on TV.

The only trouble was, a friend and I rigged the contest. We copied students' signatures on a mimeograph machine. Eventually, of course, the Powers That Be caught us. They addressed the issue quietly since they'd embarrassed themselves on TV. Eventually they laughed about it, saying, "Aw, Joey, you're such an asshole."

That experience should've taught me not to be a con artist. But I didn't learn, as you'll see later. I didn't learn from a lot of stupid tricks I pulled.

Like the time when I was 16 and I decided to have a cigarette in the house. I got brave, and I pulled out my pack of Pall Malls. That was the time when you rolled up the cigarette pack in your tee-shirt sleeve. But you didn't do it in front of your folks.

So there I was, sitting next to my dad after he came home from work—he was all greasy from working in the junkyard he owned. He sat on a towel on the couch so he wouldn't get grease all over it. He turned on the TV, put a toothpick in his mouth, and sat casually with his hands clasped behind his head.

At the first commercial break, he lit up a cigarette—he smoked Luckies. I reached for my pack, pulled out a Pall Mall, and lit it. Unceremoniously and silently, my father swung his big, strong arm across the couch and knocked the butt right out of my mouth. That was the last time I ever smoked in front of my father.

But I kept smoking everywhere else. Finally, about 20 years ago, I wised up and quit.

My dad died from lung cancer about 10 years ago. On his death certificate it says: "Cause of death: Smoking." First time I'd ever seen that.

My mother is still going strong. She continues to save all my press clippings, which may be a sign she's got early Alzheimer's—she's forgotten I'm a pain in the ass.

found cigarettes in the house the other day. They're my ex-wife's, but my 13-year-old daughter moved them to her room. An older boy is calling her. She's flunked private school and wants to go to public school now. If this didn't sound so familiar, I'd probably just hand her over to a cult.

I recently enrolled her at The DeSisto School in Massachusetts, which acknowledges that parents, however unwittingly, can be partly to blame for their kids' learning problems. This means that the kids can't get expelled from the school, but the *parents* can.

My daughters are opposites. Kristen is a very responsible young lady, and Mercedes is a rebel like me. My ex-wife says, "Well, the world will teach her." But I'm not of the persuasion to let the world teach her. I want to do it. After all that I've been through, I'm not willing to let her go.

Everything that she's doing now reminds me of me, so I'm trying to treat her how I would've liked to have been treated. I'm trying to teach her lessons so that she'll learn them now, instead of years later, the way her dad did.

It's not easy. Nowadays, we're sucked into a system that has mentoring programs instead of parenting. Parents would rather work and pay the mortgage on a second home than raise their kids. But if *you* don't raise your children, the streets will raise them for you. Or worse—radio will.

CHAPTER 2

Radio Daze

Hiya, hiya, hiya!

—My on-air greeting in the Sixties

Even though I won, however dubiously, the Announcer of the Future contest, it didn't exactly open doors for me. You don't just go from winning a contest to being on TV full time. Someone at the station advised me, "Hey, Pinto, why don't you start out by selling time in radio?" (That's right, I was born Joey Pinto. I'm *not* going to tell you what my nickname was.)

To break into the media business, you have to go in little steps. And back then, we didn't have internships. We had "hang-around-and-be-a-pain-in-the-ass-until-someone-gives-you-something-to-do-ships." If you hung around long enough, they knew you were serious and would give you little jobs to do. People would ease you in. That's how the game was played.

One of the places I used to hang around was Buffalo station WBNY. The program director, Arnie Schorr, never did hire me, but he gave me some life-changing advice. One day he told me, "You can't use the name Pinto. It's too ethnic. You need a white bread, all-American, household name, like Reynolds Wrap. Joey Reynolds. That's it!"

So I took my new name and went to the local top radio station that played rock 'n' roll. Although it was a renegade station because it played that kind of music, it was also the foreign language station. I was given the job of spinning the foreign language records and doing the remote broadcasts for the Polish and German shows. And they let me sell ad time and keep a percentage of whatever I sold.

At 15, I got my first promotion idea. I thought, let's take the afternoon franchise man, Guy King (who now goes by his original name,

Dick Purtan, and is the number-one morning guy in Detroit), and do the show from the beach in Canada. That meant going through the Canadian government because it's their air. We didn't have the sophisticated satellite systems we have now; we had only the telephone lines and what they called a MARTI unit to relay the transmission.

I wrote a letter to the Canadian government ipso facto: "We are going to commence our broadcast on July 1 to celebrate Dominion Day and continue through July 4, our American holiday. We will have a fireworks display to co-celebrate our holidays." I copied the FCC. Everybody signed off on it like it was a matter of fact, and I began to sell the time and get sponsors.

We then proceeded to do the show from the beach all summer long.

Rigging the Announcer of the Future contest should've taught me a lesson. Instead, it just turned me into a hardened con artist. I took a tape of a disc jockey I liked in Buffalo—his name was Jerry Stevens—and sent the tape to a little station in Cleveland. And they hired me.

But when I got to Cleveland I found out that *they* had conned *me*. The station was actually 45 miles from Cleveland, in Ashland, Ohio. I took a cab and almost went broke. Because I felt deceived, I said, "You know, that's not really my tape."

And they said, "Well, we never actually listened to it."

They hired me just because they needed a warm body for $60 a week. I ended up doing the farm report, the stock market report, the Polka Hour, Candlelight Melodies, and a rock 'n' roll show in the afternoon. Back then, DJs used to work eight hours and would do whatever was in front of them. Stations broadcast all these different shows—they hadn't adopted single formats the way they have today.

I was there about a year, during which time I started sending tapes—this time, my own tapes of me doing the Top 40 music show—to every station I could think of. I used my natural voice; I didn't try to have an announcer's voice. That limited my appeal because the really good stations wanted announcer types. And when the all-Top-40 stations emerged, they wanted that real big Top 40 voice, like "Hey cousins! This is your Cousin Brucie!" I didn't have that either.

Radio announcing was an art. I was too natural sounding. My voice wasn't cultivated. I didn't know about the WOR announcer's guide—most announcers who are worth anything at all follow the WOR announcer's guide. Milton Cross, Walter Winchell, Don Pardo—all these guys were very articulate. They oozed class. They used no colloquialisms and had complete command of the language. Enunciation was everything: They pronounced every consonant of "Rimsky-Korsakov," and they said it like they meant it.

I didn't even qualify for an entry-level announcer's job, which was to give station IDs:

"You're listening to WOR, 710 AM, New York."
You had to have a certain voice for that. And I
didn't.

Nevertheless, someone at WAME ("the WHAM-
MY in Miami") liked the tape I made in Ashland
and hired me. What I didn't know was that the
guy in Miami was the same guy who used to own
a station I hung around at in Buffalo—he changed
his name from Leon Wysetewski to Leon Wilson.
And he didn't know I was Joey Pinto because I
had changed my name to Reynolds. So when we
met, we looked at each other and howled.

Leon put me in the news department as an
assistant to Larry King, who did the morning
show. Believe it or not, Larry was a great comic.
He broadcast a remote show from a booth in
Wolfie's on Collins Avenue. He had a character
named Captain Wolfie, the Crooked Cop. He
would stop people and take bribes.

Howard Cosell was a different personality
altogether. When he and Chris Schenkel came
down from New York to cover the Johannsen-
Patterson fight, I was assigned to be their assistant. Howard arrived in Miami and his ego had

to come in on a separate plane. I had to work with him for a couple of weeks to get all the fight stuff in order. I thought the way Howard used to bark at everybody was funny. He was a tall, pushy guy who steamrollered over everyone to get whatever he wanted. I had never met any-one like him.

We went to the boxers' training camps, and I brought the tape recorders and carried Howard's things and ran his errands and drove him around. He was very demanding, precise, and extremely professional. But a pain in the ass.

When he was leaving to go to the airport on his last day in Miami, he didn't have a flight reserva-tion. He walked up to the Eastern counter and said, "I'm Howard Cosell, *Speaking of Sports.*"

And the agent said, "I'm sorry. We don't have any seats."

"Well, bump someone!" Howard barked. "I am the king of sports."

And the agent said she couldn't do that. So he asked for a supervisor, and he got pissed off at that person, too. So then he went to the United counter.

All this time I'm standing there holding his vicuna coat while he's ranting and raving about how important he is. United said they'd put him on standby for a flight, but that wasn't good enough for him—he wanted first class, even if it meant having to physically push somebody off the plane.

Finally the airline accommodated him. There was stammering and screaming, but they put him on a plane. Of course, in all the frenzy, Howard left his coat behind with me. He was in such a tizzy, he forgot it.

When I got back to the station, I got a call from Howard, who was frantic when he arrived in New York, where it was 30 degrees. He said, "Joey, this is Howard. Where is my coat?!"

I said to him, "What coat?" to make him crazy.

And he said, "I had a coat, I had a vicuna coat!" He ranted and raved about the coat.

I said, "I don't know what you're talking about, Howard. I never saw a coat. You never wore a coat—you were in Florida." So I further aggravated him until he was frothing at the mouth—I could just picture him.

Eventually he said, "You're puttin' me on!"

"Yeah," I said, "I've got it in the car."

"Well, get it out of the car! It's got to be sent to me post-haste. You have to put it on the next plane to New York."

I said, "Yeah, I'll give it its own seat! If *you* couldn't get on the plane, how's a *coat* going to get a seat?"

So he said, "You're impossible, Joey! Is Chris Schenkel still there? Have him take it on the plane with him."

When I saw Howard again, a couple of years later in New York at WABC, he said, "Thanks for the coat."

From there, I worked at an alphabet soup of radio stations—WPOP, WIXY, WNDR. And what hampered me in the beginning started to work for me. People responded to my natural voice and easy-going style. Kids liked me because I was one of them, playing their music. And I was always pulling pranks.

In my early 20s, I got an offer to work at WDRC in Hartford, Connecticut. It didn't take long for me to become number one in the ratings. I was on the air from 6:00 to 9:00pm, Monday through Friday. It was an ideal shift.

I probably played more pranks than records, though. One night I was playing the Wilson Pickett record, *In the Midnight Hour*, and it started to skip, playing "In the midnight . . .in the midnight . . . in the midnight . . . " So I let it go like that for a half hour, then an hour, then two hours . . . . And for all that time I had locked myself in the studio.

The police came by because they were getting so many calls from people who thought I'd died or had a heart attack or something. The police broke the door down to get in. They expected something terrible, but there I was, grinning and playing the record. They wanted to arrest me. I put it all on the air so everyone could hear the cops coming in to reprimand me. The station got in a lot of trouble for that, but the ratings skyrocketed.

With enough pranks like that one, the station became number one and made a lot of money. The owners decided to move the station downtown, to a beautiful new 15-story building. WDRC was called "The Big D," so they built the building in the shape of a "D." But who the hell would ever know that except for helicopter pilots?

The station threw itself a moving party—it was literally a moving party because it was a parade. At the head of the parade was Petula Clark singing *Downtown*, because that's where the station was moving. The disc jockeys, who were all very popular, followed behind her.

But the one mistake they made with this new million-dollar headquarters was that they put the bathroom on a different floor from the studio. You'd think they'd put the toilet next to the studio, but you actually had to take an elevator—you couldn't even take the stairs because they were alarmed. Once, during a commercial break, I went to the bathroom and got stuck in the elevator coming back up to the studio. So I used the elevator phone and went on the air from there.

That wasn't the first time I got trapped outside the studio during a show. A girl from Southern New England Telephone Company, a.k.a. SNETCO, used to call me every night. We'd flirt with each other on the phone while the records were spinning. I thought she had a sexy voice and she liked mine, though we hadn't met. So one night we arranged to meet each other. SNETCO was just a couple of blocks down the street from the station, so she was going to go down to the street during her 15-minute break, and I was going to run down to the street during a song. We planned to say hello real fast and then go back to our corners.

So I put on the longest album I had (it was a Harry Belafonte record), and ran downstairs, without realizing I had locked the door behind me. When I saw her, I shrieked, because she was ugly as sin. It's a good thing the feeling was mutual. So she ran back to the phone company and probably locked herself in her room. But I couldn't get back into the station because I forgot my key.

I was only in my early 20s, so these sorts of things just rolled off me. But along with resiliency, youth breeds arrogance—and I was very arrogant. I would say anything on the air I wanted to. For instance, the mayor of Hartford at the time, Ann Ucello (who happened to be the first female mayor in the country), came into the station one day when I was on the air. I saw her in the hall, and I said, "Ann, come on in and talk to me!"

She ignored me. So I knocked on the glass, "Hey, Ann, come on in!"

But she walked by me. I said, "Aw, she's a dumb broad."

I got suspended for one month without pay. When my month was up, I turned the mic on at six o'clock, played my theme song, and said, "This is Joey. And she's still a dumb broad."

The owners let it slide.

LET SLEEPING DOGS LIE

*W*hen I was a DJ in Hartford, the recording industry considered the city a tertiary market. Smaller cities were test markets for new songs, so that stations in primary markets, like New York and Cleveland, would never have to waste time experimenting with new records—they'd play only those songs that had become hits in the test markets.

The official publication that tracked record performance in test markets was the *Gavin Report*. When I was in Hartford, the music director who reported the hits directly to Bill Gavin was Bertha Porter. She was a heavy-set woman who wore polka dot dresses that always seemed to have a chowder stain in the same spot.

One night she was asleep in the music library, and I took my mic and put it under her chin. Between songs, I broadcast her snores — running commentary from one of the industry's big-time music mavens.

It's a good thing she was a sound sleeper.

W hen I was looking for a place to live in Connecticut, I looked in West Hartford, which is very exclusive. I saw a quietly nestled colonial house with a little apple and pear orchard on the property. The house was being sold by a rich guy named Larry Vineberg, who built a replica of the *Santa Maria* for the '64 World's Fair and sailed it here from Europe. The novelty lasted about an hour, so he went bust with it and needed to sell some of his toys. But he wouldn't sell the house to me unless I agreed on one condition: I had to take on his longtime maid, Lily, who had spent 30 years with his family.

If anyone was more independent and arrogant than I was, it was Lily. When I met with Vineberg about the house, *she* interviewed *me* as to whether I was deserving of living in *her* house. And then she told me her terms.

"Well, now, Mr. Reynolds," she said, "I wants the followin': You'll pay me a wage of $65 a week.

You'll pay for my dry cleanin' and my car. I will have all the food I want, and I will bring it to my room if I choose to."

"You'll do the laundry?" I asked.

"I do not do laundry."

I said, "Well, are you going to wash the floors?"

"I don't do floors."

I asked, "Are you going to do the gardening?"

"I don't do gardenin'! We have Bob—he come in once a week and do gardenin' and the plowin' in the winter."

"Well," I said, "Are you going to make the beds?"

"No, sir."

"Well, what do you do?" I asked.

"I dust."

Lily got my number right away, and she was going to play me for all she could.

One day I bought a nice steak. (Lily instructed me which butcher to go to, of course.) I put the steak on the grill, and I cooked it. (Lily didn't cook either, though once in a while, she'd make duck. From my duck pond.) When the steak was done, I put it on the counter while I went to wash my hands. When I came back, the center of the steak was gone. Lily had cut around the best part, the tenderloin, and taken it up to her room.

I went upstairs, and she was sitting there with a do-rag on, eating my steak.

I said, "Excuse me, that was my dinner!"

"Well, we're family."

I said, "You're eating the best part of the steak!"

"Well, wouldn't you want your sister to have the best part of the steak?"

"You're not my sister," I pointed out.

"Honey, *you* play the records—they say you're my brother and I'm your sister. Get over it."

She also had a mysterious boyfriend.

"I've got to go see A.C.," she'd say.

"Who's A.C.?" I asked.

"He's my boyfriend."

I said, "What's his name?"

"Them's his name."

"What do you mean, 'Them's his name'?"

"Them's his initials."

I said, "Well, he's got to have a name."

"Well, I call him A.C. His name is Bob."

I said, "Then why do you call him A.C.?"

She said, "Honey, I don't ask questions of A.C. That's why we have a long-time friendship."

"Well, what do you do with him?" I asked.

"I go over on Sunday," she said. "He's my honey and I snuggle with him, and on my day off I make him dinner."

I said, "You do more for him than you do for me!"

"Well, you ain't givin' me dick."

I guess she had a point. I was hoping to meet A.C. when I threw a Christmas party one year. I invited all the people from the radio station. King Curtis (who's now in the Rock 'n' Roll Hall of Fame) came over, and a really great singer named Toby Legend performed. Lily decorated the house to a tee. She really knew how to get things done. By that I mean she knew how to hire caterers.

But A.C. never showed. After dinner, I think I heard her throw a duck back in the pond.

I hit the big time in the early 1960s when I was at WKBW, back in my old hometown of Buffalo. The station had a 50,000-watt transmitter, so folks as far away as Philadelphia, Washington, DC, and Montreal could pick us up. We actually made the ratings in some of those cities! And back then, there were fewer stations (FM hadn't opened up yet), so we had a 60—sometimes 70—share, which is unheard of today. Now, a station's lucky to get a 3 share.

I was a real original back in those days. I pioneered this natural-voice, say-whatever's-on-your-mind style of radio. I certainly wasn't an announcer, and I wasn't even "jocking," which meant hitting the cues on the records and introducing them the way Dan Ingram does—always very joyfully. I wasn't always joyful. I was just me.

Occasionally, I would insult the guests. After interviewing Brenda Lee, I made a little comment about her over the intro to a record. I said, "You know, Brenda has acne." That was pretty rude then. Not that it wouldn't be rude now, but it's pretty mild by morning zoo standards.

Maybe it was because of that my popularity grew faster than my bank account. It took me a while to realize that the station was making a lot of money off me, but it wasn't exactly being generous with it. I didn't know how to value myself or demand pay commensurate with my ratings. But I got a little lesson about that from Kelly Isley, one of the Isley Brothers.

Here's what happened: As the hottest jock in the country, people would often ask me to help them put concerts and tours together. One day, my friend Fred Klestine, who did a midday show on WKBW and whose niece went to Buffalo State Teachers College, told me that the school wanted to have a concert in its auditorium. As a favor to him and his niece, he asked me if I would be able to get the school an act. The college had a limited amount of money—about $2,500.

I made a few calls and found out that the Isley Brothers (*Twist and Shout*) were in the area on tour with the Shirelles (*Will You Love Me Tomorrow?*), Ruby and the Romantics (*Our Day*

Will Come), the Exciters (*Tell Him*), and an opening band. The whole tour had a night off, so I
called them and asked if they would like to do
the gig. They said sure.

So Freddie and I set it up with the Buffalo
State College—we got all the contracts in order.
The school was real appreciative and offered me
$500 to emcee it. So I was happy that in addition
to having some fun, I was going to make some
money.

At the last minute, the opening band that was
traveling with the tour couldn't make it. So we
came up with $500 for a local pick-up band.

The auditorium was filled. After the opening
band went on, the Isley Brothers came over to me
and said that they were not going to go on
because they needed to have half their money up
front. So I said, "Well, we'll get it to you after the
show."

They said, "No, we have to have it now. We
don't go on without our money."

I said, "What are you talking about?"

Kelly Isley pulled me aside and said, "We get
our money up front."

"Well, this is a state school," I said, "I don't think the check's going to bounce."

"That isn't the point. We get our money up front. And we have to have cash—we don't work on checks."

I said, "Well, Kelly, I'd have to go make a lot of changes."

"Well, then, you gonna have to make changes."

"But this puts me in a really bad spot," I said.

"This is the way we do it," he informed me calmly. "We don't take the money in back, we take it up front."

So I said I'd see what I could do. I went to the school representative, and he had to go wake the bursar and then the dean, and they all were mad. And the kids were stomping their feet, impatient for the Isley Brothers. Finally, we got them some cash, they went on, and it was a great concert. The entire student body was rockin'.

After the show, when Kelly Isley and I were on our way out, I asked the dean of students where I could pick up my money. The dean said, "Well, Joey, we don't feel compelled to pay you."

I said, "Why not?"

He pulled out the contract and said, "Well, you said here you'd have the Isley Brothers, the Exciters, the Shirelles, and Ruby and the Romantics."

I said, "Yeah..."

"But, uh, you didn't have the opening band, Joe and the Four Shits."

I said, "Well, it's because we used Jack and Mary Lou Sixpack."

"But you don't understand," he said. "You didn't live up to your contract."

I was dumbfounded. I said, "Well, that was just a pick-up band. We got a band—you had a band."

He said, "Well, legally, we don't have to give you the money."

So Kelly turned to me and said, "You shoulda got your money up front."

After that, I got to thinking about money. I realized I was the number-one disc jockey in America, and the station wasn't paying me anything—maybe $300 a week. Plus, I had a TV show on Saturday that the station was making a lot of money from. (My TV show was a variety program. I presented a lot of different artists and did some comedy. It wasn't a very good show, but it was successful. It got high ratings and sold out its 18 commercials.)

Anyway, I thought I was terribly underpaid and that they needed to kiss my ass and give me a lot of money and that would make me very happy.

So around this time there was a telethon for the Variety Club. People thought that because it was a fund-raising event, the stars did the telethon for free. But it didn't work that way.

Frank Gorshin, The Riddler on *Batman*, was hired to come in to do the telethon. So was Forrest Tucker, Sarge from *F-Troop*. I contributed airtime on the radio to promote the telethon, and organizers scheduled me to appear on the telethon in the middle of the night—which I thought was a little disrespectful considering my popularity. In those days, when I felt cheated and frustrated, I tended to drink.

So one night, after I had had a few drinks, I had Frank Gorshin on the radio. Gorshin, who was known for doing great impressions, wouldn't do any impressions for me. He said, "I'm here for the Variety Club Telethon," and then he went like state's witness on me.

I said, "Well, how about a little fun? Do your impression of . . . "

"I don't want to."

"How about Kirk Douglas?"

"No," he growled. He said, "Well, we're raising money for . . . "

And I said, "Yeah, of course, I know you're raising money, but aren't you going to do anything entertaining?"

I was aggravating him. I always liked him, I thought he was a great impressionist, but he was very adamant about not wanting to work with me. I kept pushing him and he didn't want to be pushed, so he walked off. I made a little comment on the air. I said, "Well, you know, he's not doing this for free. They pay him to come in for the telethon, and the guy doesn't want to work on the radio because he's too *important* for radio—he's doing television. Same with Forrest Tucker. They give him 10 grand and a case of booze in his dressing room" (which happened to be the truth).

Boy, the management went crazy when they heard that I revealed how much the guys were being paid and what their conditions were.

I said on the air, "You know, there's a company out of Pittsburgh that puts these telethons together, and it makes more than the charity. So your little donations, your bowling money, goes to those guys."

The vice president of Cap Cities, a bald guy named Bob King, came into my studio. He said, "You know, these are my friends. You insulted my friends."

And I said, "Well, I'd be your friend, too, for 10 grand and a case of booze."

He said, "I ought to fire you."

"You're not my boss."

He said, "Well, then, your boss is fired."

"Why don't you fire everybody?" I said. "You couldn't grow ratings any more than you could hair."

He stormed out. I knew I was through there.

After I got off the air that night, I had a few more drinks with the go-go girl I was seeing. Then I showed up to do the telethon. There was a crowd waiting to see me—people were clamoring all over me. Teenagers always wanted to hold onto me and have me sign autographs. After my telethon appearance, the same screaming crowd was outside. But because of the comments I made earlier on the radio, management decided to have me escorted out of the studio. So here I drew all these adoring fans, but the owners were escorting me out like a criminal. It was bizarre.

I didn't need to hang around for any formal firing. The next day I went back to the station to get my things. On my way out, I took off my shoes and nailed them to the station manager's door with a note: "Fill these."

My wildest ride was probably at WXYZ in Detroit around 1966. There was never a dull moment in Detroit. At least what I remember of it.

I lived at the Detroit Athletic Club, and my manager, Tony Mamarella, got me the first Mustang with a metal-flake paint job—Ford made about 25 of them for display in airports. He thought I should be a real local hero, driving around in Motown's prize car.

I had the freedom to play whatever I wanted on the air. And if I played a record, it became a hit.

I also had a lot of freedom off the air. Too much freedom. I drank a lot of scotch and smoked a lot of pot and screwed a lot of girls. I went drinking every night after I got off the air. I wound up in strange beds in strange places, like boats on the Detroit River. I'd wake up in the morning and forget where I was and how I got there. It was the beginning of my alcohol addiction.

After some events I've no doubt blocked out, I wound up at WIBG, which in the late Sixties was the number-one station in the Philadelphia area. WIBG used to stand for "I Believe in God." When I got there, it stood for "I Believe in Greenbacks."

The politics there were staggering. I went out with the afternoon guy who told me to avoid the morning guy. I went out with Hy Lit who said, "Whatever you do, stay away from Joe Niagara." I went out with Joe Niagara who told me, "Hy Lit's treacherous. And watch out for George Wright ..." Everybody was cutthroat.

That's because everybody was a star—WIBG was one of the few personality stations in the country. The disc jockeys had a helicopter to get them to record hops. There were lots of events to go to because Philadelphia's rock culture was stone solid.

For being on the cutting edge of music, though, the city was locked in a time tunnel.

When I landed in Philly on an American Airlines flight, I grabbed the stewardess' microphone and said, "Welcome to Philly. Set your watches back a hundred years." It's one of those cities where nothing changes. I think they're still making those cheesesteaks from the same calf.

People in the entertainment industry don't like to leave the city. They go away and make their movie or record, but they always come back. A lot of recording stars at the time—Frankie Avalon, Fabian—came from South Philly. But I was always a wise-ass. I said the best thing to come out of South Philly was the northbound train. It didn't endear me to the locals.

But that didn't matter—I was uniquely positioned to have my friends fly in from out of town. The house I had outside Philly, in Bluebell, was right next to Wing's Field and had its own landing strip. The manager of the station I had worked at in Hartford, Dick Korsen, used to land his plane in my backyard. So did Frank Kingston Smith, a radio guy whose father was the president of the American Pilot's Association. Frank came in on his plane and would take me on short trips, to Atlantic City, for instance. And a lot of recording stars would come to my house and party. Minnie Ripperton, then with the Rotary Connection, often came over from Chicago. Wolfman Jack came to visit—we became good friends. He was totally whack. We would all smoke pot around this big, roaring fireplace in the den. And it seemed we always had a kettle of lobsters on. I led a pretty decadent life, partying and bellowing at the moon.

But for such a wild guy, I had a gentleman's farm. As Lily came with the house in Hartford, a herd of animals came with the house in Philly. It started with a horse. Then Johnny Bond, who was baseball Hall-of-Famer Roberto Clemente's promoter, gave me a Great Dane. Then someone gave me some chickens. They would sleep in the trees, so when they laid eggs, the eggs would fall and splatter on the ground. I couldn't get them to roost in the garage, so I let them roam free.

Nick Virtu gave me a pet pig, which grew from 20 pounds to 400 pounds.

And then the incident occurred—the Great Dane attacked the pig. I called the vet and said, "The pig is bleeding profusely from her ear."

He told me, "If the pig is still alive, she's smarter than the dog."

I said, "You're kidding."

"No, Great Danes are inherent wild boar hunters," he said. "Hold the pig on your lap and give her a cold compress and talk gently to her."

I said, "I don't want to sleep with her, I just want to stop the bleeding."

He said, "Well, that's what you do."

So I did it and, of course, she became a part of the family. She was smart and gentle and knew how to make it on the paper. (Yes, you can potty train a pig.)

Eventually, I had to slaughter her. But I couldn't eat the meat. I'd look wistfully at it in the refrigerator . . . and though the pork chops brought a tear to my eye, I somehow managed to work my way through the bacon.

Learning to love all those animals must've gotten into my genes. My daughter Kristen's going to study marine biology, and Mercedes wants to be a zoologist. They both ride horses, and Mercedes has a cockatiel (which she won't put in a cage), two dachshunds, hamsters, and a turtle. The gentleman farmer now lives in a petting zoo.

RATS IN MY ROOM

No, I'm not talking about the hit novelty song fellow jock Danny Neaverth and I recorded when we were at WKBW in the early Sixties. I'm talking about record company rats.

Over the years I've been quoted as saying both that I took payola and that I didn't take payola. So I want to clear that up.

When record company guys offered to take me out to lavish dinners, or provide a star for a record hop, or send me to a concert, or give me cigars, steaks, or booze—yeah, I accepted those gifts. But I never took cash.

Giving gifts and going on junkets—those things are still going on today, only it's usually the program directors, not the DJs, who are being schmoozed. This sort of thing happens in every business, not to mention in politics.

But that doesn't mean I was never offered cash. When I was at a station in Hartford, Connecticut, before I hit the big time, I was pretty naïve. There was a record company guy who used to come to my studio while I was on the air and bring his company's latest record with him. If I liked it, I'd play it.

Once he gave me a record I liked so much I played it twice. While it was spinning, he asked me for a cigarette, so I handed him my pack of Salems. We talked about having lunch sometime, and on his way out, he left me a couple copies of the record.

Later, I went to get a cigarette and there was a roll of money in the pack. I was nervous—no one had ever given me cash like that. I went to the general manager of the station, explained what happened, and gave him the cigarette pack with the money in it. He said he would take care of it.

It dawned on me later that the station manager probably just took the money himself and never said anything to the record guy.

After that, I never took money. I never felt the need for payoffs. I loved my job.

I think that's why record people still like and respect me, because they know that I'm an honorable person and that I never had my hand out back in those days.

These days, being in talk radio, I don't get offered much of anything. You know what they say — talk is cheap.

CHAPTER 3

A Mouthful of Rain

**Let a smile be your umbrella . . . but
don't get a mouthful of rain.**

—My on-air send-off during the Sixties

When I was at WIBG in Philly, I had an idea to change the radio station jingle—that's the melody a station's call letters are sung to. I figured that the jingles were in the way, that people thought of them as an interruption, as a song they didn't want to hear.

So instead of singing the station call letters to the tune of the jingle, I sang them to the melody of one of the current hit songs. Then I played those call letters over the intro to the song. That meant that during the intro of, say, *My Sweet Lord,* you'd hear "I-B-G," or whatever the station's call letters were. Instead of jingles, they were called "mingles," because they mingled with whatever song was being played.

The advantage of mingles was that every time a radio station played the record with the mingle, the call letters would register in the listeners' minds as part of the song. Then, when they heard the song without the call letters on another station, they'd still hear the letters in their heads. They might even say, "Hey, we've got the wrong station on!" I thought that'd be a clever way of promoting the station.

I brought this idea to my employer. He hated it. He didn't want to spend the money on recording a new mingle every time a new song climbed the charts.

But I really believed in my idea, so when I went out to Los Angeles for a radio convention, I tried to see Bill Drake, whose company, Drake/Chenault,

programmed all of the RKO radio stations. Drake
was the man who invented BOSS radio, which was
actually a destructive force as far as personality
radio was concerned. Although BOSS radio maxi-
mized the music, it cut disc jockeys' comments to
only need-to-know information. While it forced
DJs to be very clever in short spaces of time, it
killed what guys like me were doing, which was to
be friendly and personable and chatty. But at the
time, I thought if Drake wanted to be efficient and
maximize the music time, he'd love my idea of
incorporating station jingles into the songs.

I tried to catch up with him at the convention,
but he wouldn't see me. "Too busy," he said. So I
hung around Martoni's, which is the bar where he
(and everyone else in the music business) used to
go to drink. But he always had an entourage, so
he still wasn't accessible.

My next plan of attack was to go right to his
office. I found out it was in Topanga Canyon, and
I showed up in the reception area and waited. And
waited. And waited. The receptionist said he was
too busy to see anybody.

Well, I figured, sooner or later, he must have to
come out of his office to use the men's room, so I

hung out at the water fountain outside the restroom door. Eventually, he went in, and I followed right behind him. I had a tape recorder with samples of my mingles. I stood next to him at the urinal and said, "Here, listen to these." And I pushed the play button.

A stunt like that could've easily gone the wrong way. Fortunately, it went in my favor. Drake liked them. He took me back to his office and we made a deal right then. He wanted me to produce mingles for all his RKO stations.

I was so excited I never even bothered to call my boss in Philly to tell him I was quitting. In fact, I didn't even fly back there—I just sent a moving truck and a bunch of people to move my things. But by the time they got there, my things had already been moved—someone who figured I wasn't coming back had robbed my house.

started my own company, Joey Reynolds Associates, to produce the mingles. Although they became very popular, not everybody liked them.

One night I was at a party at Martoni's, and Harry Nilsson came up to me. Like everyone else there, he was three Brandy Alexanders to the wind.

He said, "You're the guy doing those shit jingles."

I said, "Yeah, so?"

"You're ruining my records, man—you're trashing my performances!"

"How?" I asked.

"You add stuff over the intros," he yelled. "I go to a lot of trouble to make these records. I write and arrange them very carefully—every note and word. And you screw them up by putting some crap over them!"

"Well, listeners wouldn't ever hear your intros

anyway!" I pointed out. "If the mingles weren't there, the disc jockey would be talking over the intros!"

"Oh, no, no, no," he said. "My next record will have no intro on it, then you won't be able to screw around with it!"

Them were fightin' words, so I said, "Well, don't take a breath because I'll find a place to put something!"

The challenge was on. And you know, his next record, *I'd Rather Be Dead*, did not have an intro. It began with Harry singing and he didn't stop till the end. Score one for Harry.

Being a wise-ass, though, I butted up the call letters to the start of the song—a capella. It made him furious.

When I saw him next, I tried to appease him. I said, "The stations play the records with the call letters more often, so if it's your record, you're going to get more airplay. And that's the whole point, isn't it? It increases the chance people will hear your song and buy the record. I'm your friend, not your enemy—you're looking at this the wrong way."

But he was an artist, a purist. So he decked me.

Within a year I had the number-one radio production company. It then moved into TV, producing all the station IDs for Metromedia Television.

Eventually, film business started coming my way. MCA and Universal asked me to do the campaign for the film *Jesus Christ Superstar*. I had an idea to put a live billboard on the Sunset Strip—I planned to have Ted Neeley (who played Jesus) on the cross with a bunch of cast members around him singing. The idea, of course, was to stop traffic. In L.A., though, you really don't want to do that.

A friend of mine from Philly introduced me to Jack H. Harris, a filmmaker who produced *The Blob*. He asked me to help him produce marketing campaigns for some of his films. The first one I worked on was a John Landis film called *Schlock* (this was before Landis made such hits as *Kentucky Fried Movie*, *Werewolf in London*, and *Trading Places*).

My campaign for the movie included the slogan, "See *Schlock* and roll." The ad campaign got better reviews than the movie. For another picture, I made a trailer that showed the MGM lion yawning instead of roaring. But the MGM suits censored it.

I didn't limit myself to radio, TV, and movies, though. Once I got a call from a guy who really liked my trailers—he owned a dry cleaners next door to a pizza place in a strip mall on Santa Monica Boulevard. He said, "You're pretty good with the one-liners—why don't you come up with something for my store's marquee?"

So while he was on vacation in Hawaii, I put up the following message on the marquee: "Drop your pants here and have a piece next door." When he came back he was pretty mad. They weren't real happy in the pizza place, either.

As time went on, I did less work and more partying. L.A. was a very tempting candy store. I did some drugs, but alcohol was my vice of choice. I always had a mouthful of booze—which became the metaphorical mouthful of rain I had warned listeners of years earlier.

Drinking was getting in the way of my work. But as I saw it, work was cutting into my drinking time. Something had to go—so, of course, it was the work.

I didn't watch the company anymore. I didn't go into the office. I didn't pay attention to the business. The company needed leadership very badly, and I just wasn't there. When I ran out of money, I just closed the door. I didn't bankrupt the company, I just shut it down before any debts accumulated. I went to Hawaii for an extended vacation. Then I went to Aspen for an extended party. Alcoholism depleted my interest in doing much of anything else.

After a couple of years of vacationing and partying, I came back to L.A. and met my alter ego: Chester Pipken, a very religious, sober man who tried to help me put my life back on track. He looked like Chris Rock with an afro and a mustache. Even though we had very different lifestyles, we became great friends. He persuaded me to reactivate the mingles business on a modest basis. Chester was a musical arranger, so we went into business together.

Chester was always trying to straighten me out. He said, "The devil's got a hold of you, Joey. Gotta put an end to that drinkin'. I'll pray for you. You'll see."

Chester thought the church would turn me around. Even though he was raised a Baptist, he took me to Catholic mass every day, even when I was barely sober enough to genuflect.

You'd think a drunken wise-ass like me would make a righteous guy like Chester throw up his hands and run for the hills. But instead, Chester ran for the inner city. Trying to save my soul was such hard work, I guess he decided to do something that was less challenging. So he became the minister of a ghetto church in South Central.

The church was on the property of the old Pepperdine campus. Chester gave the abandoned campus housing to families who needed to get a start. All these people lived somewhat in commune fashion, although they had jobs in the city. Unlike most Los Angeles neighborhoods, ethnically, the people on the campus were mixed—and they were all getting along.

When Chester got married, I was in the wedding party. There must have been 20 people in it, and I was the only white guy. It was the biggest wedding party I'd ever been in—and up until then the only kind of party that didn't involve alcohol.

Chester must've kept praying for me, because I finally sobered up—albeit several years later. But meeting Chester was definitely a blessing—some of his Bible lessons stuck with me.

Like the story of David—I really related to him. David did everything wrong. He was made king and was arrogant about it. And he knew just how to "play" God—he often sucked up to Him and told Him how wonderful a God He was. In the Psalms he wrote beautifully of God—and God said, "David is a man after my own heart!"

But David was always honest enough to admit that he was a sinner and exemplified the worst human faults.

Then there's Adam. The difference between Adam and David is that Adam said, "It was her." David said, "It was me."

The first human error is to blame. It's what kids do when they've done something wrong and get caught. Because they're scared, they blame someone else. Adam blamed Eve, which was pretty dumb—it's not like he had any other friends there to fall back on.

So looking back, I choose to be more like David than Adam. I realize I don't have anyone to blame for my alcoholism. It was my choice. I was a willing participant—until the addiction took over my life.

**BE THE 10TH CALLER WITH THE
ANSWER TO. . . .**

Here's a little trivia question for you New Yorkers: What familiar melody is the station jingle "Seventy-seven, W-A-B-C" sung to?

It's [*I'll Take*] *Manhattan* by Rodgers and Hart. But it's such a tiny bit of the melody that folks wouldn't recognize it unless they were really thinking about it. Jingles like this one can serve as a subliminal device to get you to associate the radio station with the city.

CHAPTER 4

Pulled from the Pitt

If a frog had wings, it wouldn't keep bumping its ass.

—Old saying

After I lost Chester to God, I went back East. I ran into a friend of mine, Seymour Abramson, who owned a radio station in Lakewood, New Jersey. He also owned liquor stores and a Dunkin' Donuts. This man was livin' my dream.

Seymour and I became partners in his little daytime station, which was at 1170 on the dial. Instead of going on the air, I decided to do the programming and create a lively, eclectic environment there. I rotated disc jockeys. I figured no one should be a morning man all of his life; each jock should have a shot at every time slot. I worked the news that way, too. News was broadcast only when it happened, and then I took it off. A working story would be reported as it was unfolding, but I ran no old news.

I probably had too many disc jockeys—I really wanted listeners to hear a lot of excitement. I staged shows at the town Holiday Inn so the audience could see the radio personalities. We had Chippendale dancers and fashion models at one event. I held a Feminine Forum, where people could discuss women's issues off the air. Those sorts of things kept us involved in the community. And I established an in-house ad agency that created ads for both radio and print.

My ambitious programming was overkill for little Lakewood, but the station covered the whole Jersey Shore. I called it "11-7 Jersey Shore" and

didn't use call letters. This was in 1976, during
New Jersey's gambling referendum, and because
11 and 7 were the hot numbers for craps, I used
dice in our logo. The little station was actually
quite successful.

It was during this time that I met Carolyn. She
was my dentist's hygienist. I couldn't believe anything so sweet was allowed in a dental office. She
was (and still is) pretty, blonde, quiet, unassum-
ing, and smart, with a great smile and perfect pos-
ture. She had all the qualities I lacked.

I suppose the reason I hadn't had any long-
lasting relationships with women up till then was
that I never stayed long in one job—or in one
town. No girl had been crazy enough to follow me
all over the map. But I knew Carolyn was different
when she came to visit me after I wound up in
Pittsburgh. Surely, that was love.

Taft Broadcasting, in Cincinnati, tracked me down in Lakewood and offered me a consulting job. Taft had just bought KQV in Pittsburgh, and it wanted to kick off the station right. So I abandoned the station in Lakewood, which eventually got sold to the big FM competition.

As a consulting programmer in Pittsburgh, I started the morning show at 4:00 a.m. instead of at 5:00 because it's an early-to-work town. And because the townspeople are big into bowling, I made a TV commercial for the station called "The Tomb of the Unknown Bowler," in which a bowling pin rose from the earth as people worshiped it—I played Strauss' *Also Sprach Zarathustra* (the music from Stanley Kubrick's *2001*) while the titles read, "KQV, The Mouth of Man."

The studio was situated in the window of the Chamber of Commerce building in downtown Pittsburgh, so the radio station was visible to listeners. I hired local TV weather people and put sports scoreboards in the windows.

I also hired the mayor of the city, Pete Flaherty, a Democrat, as a morning man. He came on the air between 7:00 and 9:00 on his way to work. He was billed, of course, as "The Morning Mayor of Pittsburgh." We paid him $50,000 for his two hours a day, Monday through Friday. I guess he wasn't the first DJ to show up for work in a limo.

I believe in putting on a good show and giving a lot of stuff away. Promotion is all about creating an event. At the time, though, no one was doing that much promotion during the day on an AM station—I was accused of overproducing. (I was ahead of the curve—ten years later, Rush Limbaugh would go on in middays and "overproduce" AM radio again.) The Taft guys became worried that I was a loose cannon, that I was going to blow the place up. I really started to rock the station, and they got nervous. And I'm sure it didn't help my image that I was smoking a lot of pot.

But they had already given me the keys to the store. I knew it wasn't my money, which made me even more of a risk-taker. Naturally, management was nervous. So they sent me to Washington, DC, to talk to their attorneys. I figured they wanted to buy me out of my contract gracefully. I knew I wasn't exactly their Lipton's cup-of-suit. And I was never going to be.

The law firm, Steptoe and Johnson, was the kind of establishment where you sank into the carpet and were served everything on elegant china. I sat down across from one of the lawyers who was apparently trying to determine if I was mentally ill. He looked down at me. Then he looked further down at me—at my shoes. I had my ballet slippers on—you know, very soft leather shoes without any socks. He said, "Stay out of politics."

In other words, he didn't think, by the style of my footwear, that I had any business working for such a formal company. After all, Taft Broadcasting is the house of presidents and senators—it's very conservative.

"What do you want to do?" he asked.

"I want you to give me the money," I said. "You don't want me to be here. You think I'm the wrong guy for the job, so just give me the rest of the money in my contract, and I'll go away. I'll go play."

And that's exactly what they did.

With the Taft money in my pocket, I took Carolyn to California—she'd never been there. We went to visit my friend, Harvey Cooper, who had just become the new vice president of Twentieth Century Fox. He was born to rise through the ranks—he was Napoleanic in both temperament and stature. In an instant, he could size up guys twice his height and half his intellect. The funniest man just by being himself, Harvey didn't mince words. You'd tell him something, and he'd bellow back his one-word opinion on the subject—having a conversation with him was like playing a word association game. I'd say, "Harvey, I'm going to see So-and-So."

"Pig."

I'd say, "We're going to the corner diner and . . . "

"Rathole."

I'd say, "Did you see the new Universal picture?"

"Nauseating."

It was an added handicap when he started the conversation.

I recently ran into Harvey—I hadn't seen him for ages. He was wearing a Nehru shirt, had gray streaks in his hair, and was carrying a bookbag. He wrapped up our conversation before it began: The first thing he said to me was, "So now you know what middle age looks like."

Back then, Harvey and his wife had a nice home in Woodland Hills, and Carolyn and I sat around his pool. He started sizing up my situation. He said, "You know what you've been doing wrong all your life, Joey? You let people put a collar around you, but you're an eagle. You can't put a collar around an eagle. You need to be set free to do what you do, create the way you did at the station in Lakewood or with the jingles or on the air. You need to be in your own little area, and I want to give you the opportunity to do that. Why don't you come work with me?

"I won't bring you into the company," Harvey continued. "I'll make you a consultant so you won't have to report to anybody corporate. And you can do all of my creative work for me. Whaddya say?"

So Carolyn and her brother, who lived in Ventura, flew back to New Jersey and packed her car—or what I called the '77 Samsonite because all our clothes were stuffed under the seats. She closed the apartment in Lakewood, and she and her brother drove all the way back to California.

Carolyn and I moved in with Harvey for a while and then got a wonderful condominium in Calabasas (which was a dirt road at the time, but now it's a prime spot to live in Southern California).

Before I could work with Harvey, there was a little condition I had to meet. He didn't mention it at first. Very discreetly, he took me to AA to get me sober. He said that when I dried out, he'd start giving me work.

I was ready to quit drinking. I was sick of the results—the hangovers, the blackouts, etc. And Chester had planted the seed of *wanting* to stop drinking a few years earlier, so it was time. But God, I hated the AA meetings. At first I said I'd rather drink than go to them. But then I wised up and said I'd rather *not* drink and *never* have to go to another one of those meetings. I've been sober for 21 years now.

But when you give up a buzz cold turkey, you often look for a replacement. I didn't like acid because that was too exhausting. You had to dedicate your whole day to that. I didn't like 'ludes because they made me really stupid. So I smoked more and more pot. It made me hungry and lethargic—side effects I could live with. At least pot allowed me to maintain a semblance of a life.

Finally sober, I went to work for Harvey. I rented office space downstairs at Twentieth Century Fox—it had its own entrance, off the lot. When the Fox folks got comfortable with me, they offered me a job as creative services director. I was responsible for all of their promotions. I reported to the marketing director, Arnie Orleans, who was the best boss I ever had.

Together we did the promotions for *Star Wars, The Omen, Turning Point,* and *An Unmarried Woman.* We were grinding out lots of stuff. We brought soundtrack albums back, made them an art form again. Our biggest hit was the soundtrack to *Star Wars.*

Harvey looked out for me—he was worried that I really didn't belong inside the corporate fold. When office politics looked like they were getting the better of me, Harvey said, "Joey, you've gotta stick up for yourself!"

"How?" I asked. "Tell me what to do and then I'll do it."

Harvey said, "What do you mean 'what to do'? Just stick up for yourself!"

I gave him a blank stare, and then he threw up his hands and said, "Never mind, Joey—I'll take care of it!"

My pot habit didn't escape Harvey's Napoleanic watch, but he didn't press me on it. He was quick to confront me, though, when I developed a taste for cocaine. He decided my weakness for drugs was adolescent—that I was a spoiled kid living in a candy store. So to straighten me out, he sent me to a specialist—a pediatric psychiatrist. Needless to say, it was a learning experience for both of us.

One thing I learned without the shrink's help is that cocaine is God's way of saying you're too rich. I was living as high as I was getting. I drove around in a Mercedes convertible. Carolyn and I bought an amazing house on a hilltop with a 360-degree view of Los Angeles and an indoor/outdoor pool. (The house has been used in several movies just because of the view.)

Around this time, New York record people started to migrate to Los Angeles—*Billboard* moved its offices to L.A. This influx of East Coast egos changed the dynamic of the valley. Record bigwigs were different from movie bigwigs—the two styles didn't mesh right away. The record people were eager to establish themselves among Hollywood's power brokers and celebrities, but it wasn't such a good fit. So they found their own neighborhoods, watering holes, and party spots—my house among them.

In 1978, after about a year at Fox, Carolyn and I got married. A minister performed a simple ceremony in our game room. About 100 people came—Carolyn's girlfriend from Jersey, my family, everybody from Fox. Harvey was my best man.

I was stoned. Years later, Carolyn told me that if I weren't stoned I wouldn't have married her. I said, "That's not true! I always loved you."

She said, "No, I mean, if I knew what you were like when you weren't stoned, *I* wouldn't have married *you*."

"Oh," I said.

I certainly don't regret marrying Carolyn. I would've liked to have been there for my own wedding, though. That would have been nice.

CHAPTER 5

Wayne's World

Party on ... NOT!

C arolyn and I had a great life in L.A. We had
good friends and belonged to the Bel Air
Presbyterian Church, which is the church
President Reagan used to attend. (I was friendly
with him when he was between jobs.) We had a
good spiritual life. And we always had dinner
parties because I loved to cook.

Carolyn is easy-going and loves to golf, so she
liked L.A. She went back to work as a hygienist,

and because she has such a soft touch, she was in constant demand from the L.A. dentists.

Every weekend we went somewhere. If we didn't go to Palm Springs, we would go to the mountains. We had good jobs, good money, a nice place to live, and could travel—it was just perfect. I know now that it doesn't get any nicer than that.

After three years at Fox, I went to work for Wayne Newton, whom I'd known for a while. He offered me the presidency of ARIES II, the company he wanted me to start up. The idea behind it was that while he was in Vegas, I was to set up a record company and arrange TV and movie appearances for him in L.A. Kenny Rogers was starting to make inroads in Vegas at the time, so Wayne chose to stay in Vegas to maintain his edge over Kenny.

I reported to Jay Stream, who was in charge of Wayne's affairs. A billionaire and president of the Arabian Horse Association, Jay had straightened Wayne out financially, helped him change his clothes and his act, and made Wayne a deal with Howard Hughes, whose Suma Corporation owned the Frontier, the Sands, and the Desert Inn. I think the deal nabbed Wayne a million dollars a month for the rest of his life. So while I was working for Wayne, I was really working for Suma, because Suma owned Wayne.

Jay Stream asked me if I'd rather be in L.A. or Vegas. He said, "So long as you stay out of that goddamn dressing room, I don't care where you are. You'll get sucked in if you go in Wayne's dressing room, and then you'll be as useless as a third tit."

HOLY (ROCK 'N') ROLLER

One day in Vegas, when I was playing blackjack, I happened to look up and out of the side of my eye I spotted Jay Stream standing there behind me. He said, "What are you trying to do? Give 'em back what we just took from them?"

He took me aside and said, "You know, if you want me to, I'll just take your check and deposit it directly with the casino and then Howard Hughes can have the money back. You can't beat 'em, you know. Notice *we* don't gamble . . . ."

You can bet I never gambled after that. No booze, no cigarettes—I lived like a Mormon during the time I worked for Wayne.

So I set up an office in L.A., with about 18 people working for us. Jay would fly me to Vegas on his Citation jet twice a week—it's only 40 minutes flying time. But I didn't spend too much time there. I agreed with Jay, who thought I'd be more valuable running the company away from Wayne. Wayne is a star and stars want their asses kissed all day—you can't get anything done. They change their minds every five minutes—"Buy me a hotel, peel me a grape, is there ice in that?"

Wayne was recording an album with Terry Woodford at the famous Muscle Shoals studio in Alabama, the place where artists like Aretha Franklin and The Rolling Stones made history. He did a TV special once a year, he played 36 weeks at the three Suma hotels, and he did a week-long gig in Germany. We added a stint at the Boardwalk Regency in Atlantic City. Occasionally, Wayne would do the *Tonight Show* but only when Bill Cosby was hosting. He hated Johnny Carson because Johnny implied he was gay, which he isn't. And once Johnny began appearing at the Sahara, Wayne felt competitive.

Wayne had a burning desire to own a hotel in Vegas. Jay Stream advised him against it—he

didn't think Wayne should be competing with any
of the Suma hotels, which were cutting his
checks. But Wayne was driven. He eventually built
a hotel, the Shenandoah, across the street from
the MGM. It didn't have a gambling license, so it
wasn't in direct competition with Suma.

But Wayne still coveted a piece of the gaming
action. So when Jay had a heart attack and
Wayne was left to his own devices, he made a
deal with the governor for a gaming license at
another hotel, the Aladdin. He got the license
and ownership of the hotel. It subsequently went
under. (Suma was probably never too worried.)

If Wayne wasn't born to be a hotelier, he was
born to be a host. Wayne really knew how to
throw parties. He'd let his prize horses out on the
front lawn, which was dotted with fountains. He
used to have peacocks on the lawn, too. I thought
that was a little fanciful, or maybe even a jab at
NBC, Johnny's station. But then I learned that
peacocks kill rattlesnakes. There's actually a reason to have them. On the back lawn, he'd have a
big barbecue with sides of beef and every other
side you could imagine, with a full complement of

servants and stars—including Nipsy Russell, Pearl
Bailey, and the Prince of Saudi Arabia.

Wayne was a good friend and easy to work for.
But he lived a different lifestyle. Wayne's day
began at 7:00 p.m. in the dressing room and
ended at 3:00 in the morning. He was very insu-
lated by people who would say only things he
wanted to hear—servants, bodyguards, drivers,
handmaidens. . . . This is not normal, you know.
This was Wayne's World, and it didn't involve
going to K-Mart.

Jay said to me one day, "Wayne wants to do a movie—a Western."

I said, "Is this fantasy week?"

He said, "No—he's a pretty good actor. Will you call your friends over at Twentieth Century Fox?"

So I called Alan Livingston, who was the Fox president at the time, and said, "I want to see you about Wayne Newton."

"How is Wayne?" he asked.

And I said, "Oh, he's good. Why don't you and your wife come see him sometime? In the meantime, Jay Stream wants to have a meeting. We'd like to talk about doing a picture with Wayne."

He said, "OK, set up the appointment."

So Jay and I went over to Alan's office—he had all these couches; it looked like a Levitt's showroom. Someone brought us coffee and tea. Alan said, "How are you boys? What's going on, what's happening? Joey, how do you feel?"

I said, "Fine. Wayne wants to do something. He's got an idea for a Western."

"Oh, I like Wayne, I told you that," Alan said. "He's a terrific guy. He's done some good acting and he's a wonderful singer and all-around entertainer, and we're really happy with him . . . " And he spoke of this and that and went on and on. He started talking to Jay about finances and money and investments and property and horses and sheiks and the Saudis. And then we said good-bye and left.

When we got outside, I turned to Jay and said, "We didn't make a deal with him."

Jay said, "What do you mean?"

I said, "We didn't talk about what we were here for."

"But you did make a deal."

I said, "I did?"

"Yeah, you made it in the first five minutes."

"Well, I must have slept through it then."

"No," he said, "if you don't have a deal in the first five minutes, you don't have a deal. You already made one. Just send him the paperwork for what you want. It's done."

And he was right. If you think about it, in any sale, any meeting, it either clicks in the first five minutes or it doesn't. You know right away—the rest of it is just posturing. The deal is done when you walk in and sit down and say here's what I'm here for, and that's the end of it. And then there are those people who drag out a bad lunch and never get to what they're there for.

So I sent the paperwork through, and Wayne made a Western for television. It should be so easy for the rest of us.

After working for Wayne, I hosted *Satellite Live*, the first radio show in the country broadcast live by satellite. Jeff Sudikoff, a genius from Boston, figured out how to make the government satellite installations commercial. He hooked up two shows—*Satellite Live*, a celebrity talk show, and *Rock Line*, which aired on FM stations, played music, and interviewed recording artists. My show, *Satellite Live*, was broadcast live from Hollywood on Sunday nights, 10:00 to midnight, East Coast time, and aired nationally on 60 stations.

I had celebrities in the studio, and people called in with questions. We put a computer in front of the guests—the callers' names and where they were from appeared on the screen. This was more brand-new technology at the time.

My first daughter, Kristen, was born when I started hosting *Satellite Live*. I had her on the air with me during our very first show. Tom Cruise was my guest, and when he picked the baby up, she peed on him. Kristen's never been easily impressed.

Working one night a week was pretty cushy. So I got a gig at KMPC in L.A., a legendary radio station owned by Gene Autry. The station featured a lot of television personalities—Wink Martindale, Bob Eubanks, Gary Owens, as well as Dr. Laura and Hilly Rose (who now sits in for Art Bell). The building was a block long, but it seemed about two feet narrow. You expected to walk around the corner and find two prop sticks holding it up.

I started out doing an hour-long, syndicated comedy show following the Angels games. Then Jim Davis, the program director, decided to beef up the morning show, hosted by Robert W. Morgan. He said to me, "I'll make a deal with you. We sign off the station at midnight on Sunday for maintenance, and we come back on the air at 2:00. I need someone to warm up for Morgan's morning show. I'd like you to go on at 2:00 in the morning until 5:00. You can do whatever you want to do."

So I did the Sunday night satellite show, The Joey Reynolds Comedy Hour, and this lead-in thing for Morgan on Monday mornings. My life was still pretty cushy.

Evangelist Billy Graham signed the station off at midnight on Sundays. So I got on the air at 2:00 in the morning, and I said, "We're giving away a brand new Rolls Royce! I'll take the fifth call." And the phone actually rang—three people called me! I was spooked. I didn't think anybody would listen to dead air for two hours. But some people, who must've fallen asleep with their radios on, heard that then woke up and dialed. Thank God there weren't five of them because I probably would have been taken to court.

I built a show based on whoever came in and whatever oddballs I could find—kind of like what I'm doing now at WOR. I took the attitude that people who are up in the middle of the night and the goofballs make a good match.

I had a guy on who, for alleged health benefits, drank his own urine—Matthew Katz, who was the lawyer and manager for Jefferson Starship. Some nutty nuns came on one night. They were an off-beat order—the Sisters of the Desert or something. They didn't wear shoes because they didn't believe in killing animals to provide leather. Yet they drove up in a minivan. And they were smoking something that smelled very strange. I thought it was marijuana, but it was herbs.

Doug Moody was a regular on my show. He thought rock 'n' roll had gotten very dull and had lost its bite—he wanted to restore its rebellious spirit. So he opened his studio to any groups who wanted to record for a modest fee—and who were willing to give him part ownership of their tapes. He wound up with four or five hits by local alternative artists, like The Dead Kennedys and Oingo Boingo.

Doug got me to record a song called *My Dog Sex* with the drummer Sandy Nelson, who had a hit called *Teen Beat* years earlier. So while Doug was pushing the alternative music, I was pushing the alternative talk.

At the time, Steve Allen was on Channel 5 in L.A. doing the "Man on the Street." I was more interested in doing that sort of thing than I was in doing a conventional talk show, which I abhor.

Conventional talk shows are merely family arguments, which I really don't like refereeing—it's not me. I know they're popular, but I don't care whether people get to voice their opinions when they're voicing only anger. Let 'em go in a primal scream room. I don't want that in my face all night.

Since KMPC let me to do whatever I wanted, I took a microphone and a cord—we didn't have a remote mic—and I spliced it together with another long cord and another one, until I had about 150 feet of wire. I went across Sunset Boulevard to Denny's with my mic, and I interviewed people, having fun with them in a booth, just like the "Man on the Street."

We didn't have a union engineer—our budget was pretty modest because it was an overnight show. I just had a guy who kept the transmitter on and turned on my mic when I was across the street. But one night someone drove over the cord on Sunset Boulevard. So I must have broadcast a good 15 minutes of dead air before someone told me I wasn't being heard anymore. I had no phone set-up or anything over at Denny's. I was just making it up as I went.

Robert W. Morgan came to work one day, and he said to me, "You know, Joey, you are *The Rocky Horror Show* of radio. I never know what to expect when I come in here in the morning. I see these nuns, I smell this incense, I find food all over the floor—Was there a sacrifice? Did you perform some kind of ceremony? Or did you get into a food fight with the sisters?"

NET GAIN

$\mathcal{S}$atellite broadcasts, simulcasts, computer screens displaying callers' names—we take all this technology for granted today. It's hard to remember when we didn't have cable, let alone color TV. And we'll become accustomed to the next big technology game, too—the Internet.

The Net is the CB for typists. The Internet "Good Buddy" is an anonymous screen name. But you have to know how to spell and write or you can't use the Internet. It's good to know that in a nation that's constantly fighting illiteracy (because we spell cheese K-R-A-F-T), we haven't completely dumbed down our entertainment media. To take advantage of new media, new jobs, and new entertainment, you still have to master the basics—reading, 'riting, and 'rithmetic.

Entertainment is a form of communication, and in the case of the Internet, it's two-way communication. You can be a part of it, either by joining a chat room or by posting your own Web page. (So you'd better be sharp.) And now, more than ever, we need to improve our communication skills.

Maybe the Internet is God's way of giving us another opportunity to do just that.

*S*atellite *Live* was carried on KOA radio, so I was invited to do a live overnight television show in Denver on KOA TV, which was simulcast on radio. In fact, the KOA TV show, *All Night Live*, was the first simulcast in the country. I was still on Sunday nights from Hollywood—I commuted from L.A. to Denver until I got tired of that and moved the family to Denver.

I did the KOA-TV show totally live, without a seven-second delay. In those days, the equipment used to delay sound as well as video was a Sony video multi-track recorder, which cost a million dollars. The station was not going to spring for that just to seven-second delay an overnight show. So we went by the seat of our pants without a delay.

People called in, and whatever they said got on the air. I never mentioned that we didn't have a delay—I didn't want to invite trouble. But occasionally some bad words got through—mainly from drunks who called at 2:00 in the morning when the bars closed.

I had my E.N.G. director, Haney Howell (of course, I called him "Heiny"), go to the houses of people who were watching me on television. He would bring the camera in while we were on live, and we'd see how long it would take the people to realize they were watching themselves.

Being simulcast, I had to serve two masters: radio and TV. It wasn't easy. The radio program director didn't like the visual antics we did on TV. So he always fought against our taking cameras out on the street because he thought it was too visual. He wanted me to take more phone calls. At that point, I thought radio was duller than dogshit. I wasn't interested in taking phone calls on the air. But that's the job. So I had to give up doing a lot of the visual stuff. We decided that to serve both TV and radio, I was never to acknowledge one or the other—I would just do the show. I could hold something up to the camera, but I couldn't mention it—we didn't want to bore the radio audience with things they couldn't see. So I could still have visual pranks, but they had to occur ancillary to the talk. It's a trick I learned to do pretty well.

For instance, I had shelves behind me where I placed all of the paraphernalia from every local school, club, and team. During the chat, the camera would pan across the shelves so the local TV audience had something to relate to.

It's like the *Today* show, where the camera shows the people outside—you see them standing in front of the glass watching. *City TV* in Toronto puts cameras down in the subway to pick up people's activities—you get to watch that between events in the studio. People like to watch other people, but they don't need the sound. They can be listening to something else at the same time. It's a great idea.

I don't like Don Imus and Howard Stern on TV because their shows are not visually compelling. You're just watching these two guys doing their radio shows. So what? You can listen to them while you're doing the dishes—you don't need to *watch* them.

It took a full crew of 18 people for the live show. We hadn't figured out the robot stuff yet.

And management always wound up assigning me staffers who really didn't want to be there. It was punishment to work all night—you had to have been naughty with the union to get on that shift. Invariably, the director would call for a shot and it would be out of focus because the guy was asleep on the camera.

Alan Berg, the controversial talk radio host, was a frequent guest on *All Night Live*. (Eric Bogosian's play and Oliver Stone's film *Talk Radio* were based on the book about him, *Talked to Death: The Life and Murder of Alan Berg*.) Alan was an unattractive, gnarly man whose dog—an Afghan—had nicer hair than he did. Alan, who used to be Lenny Bruce's attorney, could be as funny and cantankerous as his former client. He referred to the courtroom as a "theater of elegance." On his radio show, he would really get people going—callers would argue with him and then he'd hang up on them. I always become friends with these wild guys for some reason—I guess because they don't get to me. I'm amused by them because they're so cranky.

One night Alan was sitting on the couch next to me on my TV show, and he said that he took better care of his hooker than he did his ex-wife. He said, "I send my hookers to college. I want an educated hooker." That was his sense of humor, a little provocative and a little perverted.

Alan would go on the air and try to rile everybody up, and it worked. He was Jewish, so naturally he was vigilant for anti-semitism—eventually that talk got somebody going, somebody who took a gun and shot him in cold blood.

The week before he was killed, he was on my TV show. He made some comments about neo-Nazi idiots. And I said, "You know, if you don't watch your mouth, you're going to get killed." We laughed about it.

But after he was shot, the FBI interviewed me. I figure I must have a file.

Before GE sold KOA radio, it hired Roger Ogden, who was the general manager and boy wonder from Gannett Channel 9 in Denver, the highest rated TV news station in the country. Once at GE, Roger sold the radio station to Jacor (now the number-one company in the business).

Roger wanted me to finish my contract on TV and make a deal on my pay since I wouldn't be simulcast on the radio station anymore. I brought Carolyn and Kristen to my meeting with him and said, "Tell *them*!"

He gave me my money, and I moved the family back to L.A. I didn't do anything for a couple years after that. I lived in Palos Verdes in a 10-room villa on the ocean. I was very spoiled. Carolyn would play golf, and I would stay home with Kristen. I enjoyed carrying her around.

By the time Kristen came along, Carolyn and I had done a complete lifestyle turnabout. We didn't drink or smoke—we just ate health foods and took vitamins. We did natural childbirth. We drank purified water. We got into physical fitness.

Kristen's very mellow as a result of it. I think when you keep yourself really healthy, your child has a better chance of being a whole person physically, mentally, and emotionally.

I was also lucky to be able to spend so much time with my kids. You want your kids to know that you're there for them. But you can't expect them to fully appreciate it when they're young. Parental support is kind of like Recovery: you don't know it's there until you need it. People don't know anything is there until they need it. There's a great Chinese saying: "When the student is ready, the teacher will appear."

And there's always another teacher.

CHAPTER 6

Rockin' Around the Christmas Tree

Life is learning to accept Plan B.

When Howard Stern was fired from WNBC in New York City in the mid-Eighties, I was hired to replace him in his time slot. But even after I got there, the attention was still around

Howard. He still came to NBC studios to do David
Letterman's show, which bothered me because I
was looking for my own place at the station. I
wanted to create my own identity there, and I
thought Letterman could give me a helping hand.

NBC was trying to move away from playing
music (which it eventually did) by putting in
place personality shows, each with a team of five
people. That's what Don Imus had (and still has).
Soupy Sales had a team in the midday, and I had
one for the afternoon drive. NBC had given
Howard the team of Robin Quivers, Al
Rosenberg, Stuttering John, and Jackie the
Jokeman. Management had also given Howard a
bigger production budget than they gave me—he
had more pre-produced bits, like "Hitler's
Bunker" and Al Rosenberg's Grammy reports
from a pay phone. But NBC didn't want to go
the shock route anymore, and I no longer did the
kind of "shock jock" antics I did when I was
young. I created an environment that was cornier
than what Howard was doing.

My team included Brett Butler (who eventually
got her own TV show, *Grace Under Fire*), Bill
Scheff (who went on to write for Letterman), and

Tom Quigley (who was one of Bob Newhart's writers). My producer, Tim Wittaker, wrote for the *Philadelphia Inquirer's* Sunday edition—he covered all the show biz news and wrote a book about sports icon Jackie Robinson.

Jane Dornacker, who played the nurse in *The Right Stuff*, was my helicopter reporter. She was with theatrical rock group The Tubes in San Francisco and started out in comedy there with Robin Williams and Whoopie Goldberg. She was an extremely funny comedienne, but her life ended in tragedy. Twice she was in a helicopter crash during my show. While she was recuperating from the first accident, she still came into the studio to do her reports. (Ed Koch, who was the mayor of the city at the time, would sing and play piano in the studio with her.) After she had recovered, NBC put her right back up in the helicopter. A month later, she had another accident. The helicopter went down again, in the middle of a show. The pilot was OK, but Jane was killed.

Whoopie and Robin Williams came to the show to offer condolences, and they did a benefit for her in San Francisco to raise money for her 12-year-old. She had been a single parent.

TIME SERVED

*A*fter 25 years of service, employees of Cap Cities Broadcasting were given gold watches. Back when I was a DJ at Cap Cities' station WKBW, management knew I'd never make 25 years anywhere—they didn't even think I'd make it to age 25. But they said, "You're such a valuable employee, we're going to show you our appreciation." So they gave me a Longines gold watch—a very nice, top-of-the-line timepiece.

A few years later, the watch stopped. I was in Hartford, and I took the watch to Savitt Jewelers on Main Street. I figured it was the battery. The jeweler looked at it through a loupe and threw it back down on the counter at me and said, "Get another watch."

"What's wrong with it?"

He said, "Well, it's a cheap watch anyway. Just go make an investment—buy something nice."

I said, "That's my gold watch from Cap Cities!"

"It's not gold!" he said.

"Yes, it is," I said, "and it's a Longines."

"Is it?" He handed me the loupe.

It was a "Longoon."

Following Howard Stern, my team took the audience's imagination in another direction altogether. And you can imagine how Howard's cult fans took his departure out on me, being the next guy up.

So I was eager to make a score and get the ball rolling. I asked Soupy Sales and Don Imus about going on the *Today* show, and they said, "No, they'll come after you when they want you." Imus's position was to be yourself on the air, build an audience, and then all these other guys will come after you. They'll wait until you've built a power base. He was absolutely right.

John Hayes, the station manager, said, "Listen to Imus. He's been around for a while, and he knows what he's talking about." So although I thought Imus had screwed me out of a job at NBC years earlier, he eventually became my friend. He was also in Recovery, so we went to AA meetings together.

I've come to have a high regard for Imus; I think he's a brilliant talent. I always hated it when Howard would tear into him. Given his popularity, longevity, and contributions to radio, he doesn't deserve that. Howard would do the same to Soupy Sales—he's relentless about taking people down.

Just the other night on my show, I had on one of Roseanne's former writers (Roseanne Barr Arnold Whatever, that is), and she was talking about what a pain in the ass Roseanne is. I told her that I met Roseanne when I was on television in Denver. She came on my show, and she wore a housewife's outfit with a parka over it, she was chewing gum frantically, and she was hysterical. She was funny and nice and had a big smile and a great laugh. And here this writer was talking about what an animal Roseanne's become. So I highlighted the good times with her, because you can always look for the worst in someone—it's too easy to harp on the negative. Yet there must be a reason she is where she is. She had—and still has—tremendous appeal to people.

And so have Imus and Soupy. Imus has had a huge following, and so has Soupy Sales. I mean, why would you want to make a career of bringing these guys down? What's the point?

But getting back to WNBC, I was still looking to make an impression. Ignoring Soupy's and Imus' advice about waiting for the network shows to come to me, I tried to get on Letterman. But Letterman was kissing Howard's ass back in those days because he liked Howard's irreverence and may have sided with him over his NBC dismissal. Letterman couldn't make room for both of us. Letterman liked to be the bad boy but not get blamed, and Howard didn't mind taking the blame. (Eventually, Howard started to do what Letterman does, which is to send someone out to do the dirty work when a tough interview is about to slap him back. Now Howard sends Stuttering John out to do the dirty work. Letterman does that famously—except the one night he got caught off guard when Cher said to him, "You're an asshole.")

I was trying to get on Letterman's good side, so I went upstairs to his office and tried to make nice with him. But he wouldn't have any of it. (Paul Shaffer, on the other hand, liked me. I guess he respected my roots in rock music. He's also a fan of Frankie Valli, who wrote my theme song, so Paul wrote a theme for me, too. Frankie Valli dragged him downstairs one day to be on my show—we had a lot of fun.)

So one day, after failing again to get Letterman's attention, I took my live remote mic to where his audience queues up in the afternoon. I warmed up his audience in the lobby of the RCA Building (which is the job that Eddie Brill does for Letterman now at CBS). I handed out Joey Reynolds T-shirts that said "Hiya, Hiya, Joey Reynolds" on them. So when the audience went upstairs to the studio, everybody was wearing one of my shirts. Well, Letterman freaked, although I would have thought that was a perfect Letterman bit—it was funny and promoted the station. If it was Howard Stern, he probably would have run with it. But Letterman wasn't such a sport. He had them take the shirts off.

I was still struggling to make my mark in the shadow of everything Stern. There was Stern Jewelers, Stern's department store, the Stern financial company. Plus, I'd get all Howard's old hate mail.

So in an effort to make a mark, I once again took my microphone and went outside. It was Christmastime, and Rockefeller Center was bustling with tourists who came to see the lighting of the big tree. Brett Butler and Tom Quigley had written some "fractured" Christmas carols, which I planned to get the tourists to sing. But I made a strategic error— I didn't think it all the way through.

The network was preparing to cover the tree lighting ceremony, so there were a lot of NBC technicians around. Since I had an NBC microphone, they thought I was officially involved in the tree lighting ceremony. When I got a bunch of people to stand around and sing these fractured Christmas carols, I asked the technicians to

put the tree lights on, and they did. But when the
tree lit up, everybody who was rehearsing for the
official tree lighting show thought it was a signif-
icant part of the ceremony, and they started to
file out and do their part—including Helen Hayes
and Liberace.

I didn't realize what was going on at first. I was
surprised to see Liberace, so I pulled him aside
and said, "What's that you're wearing?"

And he said, "Oh, it's just something I had in
the closet."

I said, "Don't be silly, you haven't been in the
closet in years."

Penn and Teller were there. I tried to interview
Teller, the one who doesn't speak. David
Rockefeller, the landlord, was there, so I asked
him how much he charged for rent. I asked him
if he was bothered that his new tenants (GE) had
so many extra bulbs on the tree this year.

The network folks were incensed that I had
gotten the tree lit and moved all the machinery
into place—the band, the skaters, the celebrities. I
was laughing, but I was in trouble. It was not a
good day upstairs. It happened pretty innocently,
too. I just wanted us to sing our silly carols.

Afterwards, I went upstairs and hid from people for a few months. The next time I stuck my head out, I saw my shadow, and there were only six more weeks left of my show.

CHAPTER 7

Reynolds Rap

I trust in God. But I tie my camel.
—Old Arab saying

These days I'm doing what I really love to do on radio—talking. I'm not spinning a bunch of records dictated by the corporate playlist. I'm a personality just being myself, hanging out with a bunch of friends after midnight. I don't always know where the show is going, so it's exciting. It's got a stream-of-consciousness style to it.

I used to get busted for that easy-going style.
When I had a Top 40 countdown show at
WKWK in Wheeling, I was supposed to play song
number 40 through song number one between
3:00 and 6:00 in the afternoon. I would start
with number 40 at three o'clock and, invariably,
at 6:00 I would say, "Stay tuned for the top four
with Bill Quay." The next guy would have to play
the songs that I couldn't squeeze in because I
wanted to chat.

A station manager at WMCA, another rock
station where I worked, once said to me, "Why
don't you try doing a one-hour show instead of
six 10-minute shows?" I didn't have the continuity
he was looking for. But to me, just announcing
records was boring. It wasn't really doing anything. Living my life through recording artists was
not my goal.

With the overnight talk show on WOR, I've got
a rare freedom in this day of Top 40 and service-
oriented radio shows. Very few DJs on commercial
radio have that kind of freedom right now.
Howard Stern has to stay in the crotch or he loses
his audience. Rush Limbaugh has to make fun of

the president or he doesn't have a show. Dr. Laura's got to sit there and listen to everybody's whining. These folks don't have freedom; they're imprisoned by their narrow formats.

Do you know the difference between prison and jail? I just learned this the other day—I had never known there was a difference. Jail is the place you stay until the matter is resolved; prison is where you go as a result of your crime.

There are lot of words we just assume mean the same thing. We never stop to think about them. Like "envy" and "jealousy." Envy is wanting what someone else has. Jealousy is not wanting that person to have it. But you can't take away another person's successes, no matter how jealous you are. Jealousy will only thwart your own success.

The other day, I heard some young comedian put down Joan Rivers, who works here at WOR with me. This girl was making fun of Joan's comedy style. But she was obviously jealous of Joan. Think about it: Joan was the first female host of the *Tonight Show*. What are they going to do? Take that away from her? She had the first live show on FOX television. Gonna take that away from her? She was one of the first of the female breakthrough comics. You can't take those accomplishments away.

W hat talk radio does better than TV and movies is create a sense of intimacy between the host and the audience. Radio can be a constant companion, a real close friend. Maybe you can get more intimate on the phone, talking about your mother, or in an Internet chat room communicating with some fat guy posing as a lesbian. There's intimacy in that, I suppose.

Other media spend zillions of dollars and hours of research to figure out how to get the intimacy that a radio show is capable of. There's no intimacy on TV. You don't know anything about Jay Leno except that he collects cars. You know that Letterman gets stalked, and that Larry King has had 100 wives, and that Conan O'Brien wrote for *The Simpsons*, but that's all you know about these guys. They're in your life at least an hour every day, if you watch them, yet you know nothing about these hooligans.

Not that radio is always intimate. If a DJ is a puker on the air—"Hey, everybody, welcome to

Five in a Row!"—there's no intimacy in that. But if a DJ gets on the air with a caller who says, "Hey, you know, I'm really in trouble and I'm hurting and I don't know what to do about this, but here's what I've done so far," you could sit there by your radio all night. It'll have you gripped like no film or sitcom.

For example, the comedian Robert Schimmel was on my show a while back. He's very funny, but I didn't want him to just recite his act on my show. I wanted the audience to get to know him as a human being, apart from his act. So he told a story about his son who was 12 years old when he died of leukemia. His son had a going-away talk with him in the car one day. The boy said, "Dad, I'm sorry I'm dying because I'm sad to leave you." And Robert pulled the car over and broke down and cried. He shared that on the air, and it was a very touching moment.

On the other hand, radio can be a parasite. It does not create anything on its own. It uses other people's input—their music and stories and phone calls—to entertain its audience. It's the most boring, deadbeat, bottom-of-the-totem-pole format of all the entertainment media. It's greedy and a bloodsucker. (Except for my show, of course.)

What's more, radio is manipulated by program directors who are scared and by managers who don't want to lose their jobs. The business is fear-based. These guys are always juggling around the format to make ratings. They live and die by the numbers.

Today, choosing records to play on the air is a science. It used to be an art. Stations today play the songs that are selling, and sales are researched. It used to be that you would buy records based on what the DJ thought was good, and now it's just the record company force-feeding songs to the program directors. The DJs aren't making the hits. The listeners aren't making the hits. The record companies are dictating the hits. And they target the least discerning, most impressionable listeners—teeny boppers who don't have the attention span to listen to a DJ for more than 10 seconds.

You know what I think killed the art of being a disc jockey? What did in the great personalities back in the early days of rock? It was The Beatles. They got bigger than the jocks. The jocks weren't necessary anymore. Up until then, a guy walked into a room, played his records, and you listened to his rap. Nowadays, every station is playing the same 10 songs. And between the songs and the commercials, a DJ has about 10 seconds to cultivate a relationship with the audience, to express his or her personality. As a result, there's nobody to emcee the songs today, so, once again, the hits have to appeal to the least sophisticated listeners—teens.

It's high time Top 40 radio stations did a morning show with a real DJ who could emcee the show instead of doing schtick all the way through the morning rush. People over 25 need someone to say, "Here's such and such artist. This is what he's all about and here's what he's done." You need a Casey Kasem in the morning—somebody who could give older listeners a libretto so they can figure out what the hell the music is about. No 40-year-old who's been listening to Rush or Larry King can switch to a music station and know what's happening with Beck. They think it's a beer. They barely know Oasis, and they were Grammy winners. Why is that? Something's wrong.

Top 40 used to offer a cross section of music styles. If we had that today, you'd listen to some R.E.M. and then some Trisha Yearwood, and then

the DJ would explain that Trisha is in the Grand
Ole Opry Hall of Fame and she started out by
singing backup for Garth Brooks. And here's a little bit of Hanson, and they're 13 years old and
they're family. And now here's the Pizzicato Five—
there's actually three of them and they're from
Japan. It was the DJ's job to tell you all of that.
Now you have to watch MTV and read every teen
magazine to figure it out. Music is being so nar-
rowly marketed today that one age group, a.k.a.
"demographic," never gets to hear what appeals to
another "demographic."

Most of the FM shows come from the crotch
and the AM shows end up in the White House.
I'm trying to do mine in the living room, for a
cross-section of listeners. Trouble is, I'm not sure
American houses are being built with living
rooms anymore.

The result of our relentless catering to the demographics is separatism. We serve different age groups and give each of the age groups its own entertainment centers so that sponsors can market their goods directly. The payback for that approach to entertainment is that we lack unity.

The beginning of this target marketing craze was the decline of the Ed Sullivan format. Back then, everybody sat in the living room waiting for the act he or she liked. You had to sit through everybody else's crap to get to your crap. Nowadays, nobody sits through anybody's crap; you have only your crap because we have no cross-culture. It's very difficult for a heavy metal fan to sit through a country act. It's a considerable challenge for somebody who likes Aerosmith to watch a ballet.

The marketers decided to divide and conquer. They delivered entertainment so that a person who is 15 years old doesn't have to put up with the tastes of somebody who is 50 anymore. As a result, teenagers have lost what little respect they may have had for seniors—and, what may be even worse, the seniors have lost respect for children.

We need another Ed Sullivan or Johnny Carson—someone who can bridge the generation gaps. Unfortunately, we don't have many comedians today who could pull that off. Most comics today think that the world owes them something. They are very self-centered. Their bravado really stems from fear. They're overcompensating. A person who acts in charge and has to be the center of attention at all times is actually a fearful person. Someone's who's always afraid and on the defensive cannot be a kind, professional person.

We don't have many generous comedic personas anymore—people like Lucille Ball, Red Skelton, Jackie Gleason, Sid Caesar, and Robin Williams. You can't make me think for one minute that Jim Carrey is of their caliber and professionalism. I like his movies, and his *In Living Color* work was great—but he's not going to be the one to bridge the demographics.

Nowadays we look for smart-asses, instead of brilliance. We're celebrating mediocrity. We encouraged brilliance before; we nurtured it. We don't look for that now. Now we're just looking for whomever we can slap a label on and market for a quick buck.

Take Howard Stern. Howard has definitely established himself as a brand name. He stands for a certain something. I refer to it as "humiliation," but many refer to it as entertainment. If humiliating someone is entertaining, then he's entertaining. If being a smart-ass is humorous, then he's hysterical.

David Letterman and Howard Stern are both in the same bag: One is packaged prettily and the other one is coarse. But both of them use very adolescent humor and like to get their laughs by knocking people. I'm not saying Howard can't be really funny. When he was at NBC he was particularly creative, especially when he was doing "Hitler's Bunker" and the Grammy Award coverage. He's got a fertile imagination.

But these days, most of his humor is based on waiting for his guest to let down his guard so he can take the guy out. It used to be that comedians got a laugh by taking a pie in the face. Today, comedians like him can't be funny unless they've got someone they can throw the pie at.

I was guilty of that sort of adolescent approach to comedy when I was younger—when I myself was an adolescent. But one day the pie came right back and hit me in the face. Literally.

Here's what happened: I was at a *Billboard* convention in the early Seventies at the Plaza Hotel in New York. I was one of the most respected jocks in the country at the time because I had a huge audience. Industry people listened to what I had to say because I knew how to get ratings. One of my admirers was a guy from the West Coast, Tom Donahue. He was the father of underground radio, which focused on long-playing songs and albums—The Grateful Dead, The Who, etc. Until him, nobody was playing albums. Donahue started it on the West Coast—in New York it was Murray the K and Rosco on WOR FM. They didn't hype anything—there was none of this Top 40 frantic delivery. They played these records all the way through, said interesting things about the artists, and were very relaxed. They attracted more discerning listeners.

Tom Donahue and his partner, Bobby Mitchell, had been Top 40 disc jockeys in San

Francisco when they decided to steer away from
the common hook records and toward the likes of
Janis Joplin and Jimi Hendrix. But in doing that,
they had to change radio stations. So Tom and
Bobby went on to program KSAN, which became
an FM underground station. (They called it
"underground" because it was different. Today,
they'd call it "alternative.")

Donahue and I met at this convention, and we
had nothing but respect for each other, even
though we were doing totally different things. I
was asked to speak at the convention, and when I
got up, some guy pied me. (No, it wasn't a
cheesecake.)

Tom was pissed. He came running up to protect me. He was a big guy, maybe 400 pounds,
and tall. He went over to the guy who pied me
and said, "How dare you do that? Who do you
think you are? You're an asshole. Now, get out of
my face!"

After that, I wanted to be more like Tom and
less like the kind of guy who throws pies at
people for cheap laughs.

Now let's take Bob Hope. He was always brilliant. When I hosted *Satellite Live*, I did a one-hour broadcast from Bob's house at Christmastime. His writers didn't show up on time, but he didn't need them. I couldn't believe how sharp he was.

Years later, he was on Howard Stern's show. Howard kept trying to find an "in," to find a way to score a laugh at Bob's expense. Howard wasn't getting anywhere; Bob wasn't letting him in. Bob's no fool—he really knows how to defend himself. Obviously, Howard hadn't expected the old goat to be so sharp.

So the show was frustrating for Howard because Bob kept a safe distance. On the way out, in true Bob Hope fashion, he got the last laugh. Bob looked right into the camera and addressed the audience directly. Bob said, "Is he a fag?" He just threw Howard right to the lions.

You can't put Howard Stern in the same league

as Bob Hope. What was Howard thinking? What was he smoking that day?

Another example of this "humiliation" style of entertainment is what I call the "mob mentality." A lot of entertainers assume that all Italian-Americans are gangsters, and they think, somehow, that that's funny. But as an Italian-American, I can safely say that we're not all from Sicily, biting our hands, and swearing at dwarfs. But Joe Pesci and Danny DeVito don't mind having Robert DeNiro "mother-f" them to death. They think that's funny perhaps. I don't think it's funny. I mean, we didn't live that way in my family. I don't think New York's Mayor Giuliani comes from that kind of a family. If African-Americans don't want to see *Amos 'n' Andy*, why would I want to see *Casino*?

Nevertheless, I'm optimistic that we can find another Ed Sullivan or Johnny Carson or someone who will be able to span the demographic spectrum. We just have to be willing to nurture the talent.

And nurturing starts in our own homes. But we're bypassing the whole process there, too. We give our kids their own TV, their own cable, their own e-mail, their own credit cards. . . . We're encouraging the separatism.

The baby boomers who are enjoying the bull market are giving their kids the things that they didn't have when they were young. Giving money is taking the place of parenting. We can't just buy our kids a new video game every week and call that good parenting. What we should be spending on them is *time*.

I said to my daughter recently, "We never sit down and have meals together. You take your food to your room. Your sister goes to her room and works at the computer while she eats. And I'm the fool in the kitchen. That's not my idea of any fun. I'm very uncomfortable about it, and I'm fearful. Let's all make a plan to spend some time together. Where do you want to go?"

You've got to phrase it right and not make it a command. Say, "I'd like to spend some time with you. Do you think we could go get something to eat?" Or, "Do you think it would be OK to put some time aside?" It's all about courtesy. Kids want to be treated the same way we do. And why shouldn't they be?

'm trying to teach one of my daughters the importance of keeping her word. The other day, I said to her, "You made a plan last night. I asked you at 2:30 in the morning why you were still up when you had an appointment at the ranch at 8:30 a.m. You told me you'd go at 9:00. And here it is 10:00, and you haven't gone yet. The ranch has called and is wondering where you are."

I've made a living out of running off at the mouth, I told her, and if I've learned anything, it's how important it is to keep your word. Especially to God. After all, God keeps His word to us. He made another day, and He provided everything here. He kept His word, now you've got to keep yours. You keep your word to God by keeping it with everyone else.

My daughter's intelligent and sensitive. She heard everything I said. Does that mean she'll do it? That she believes me? I don't know. Maybe.

That's parenting. We'll learn from each other during this experience.

In fact, she taught me something pretty important the other day. We were running late for church, and naturally, I got stuck at every stoplight. I started cursing at the traffic lights and slapping the steering wheel. My daughter said, "You know, Dad, no matter what you do, you can't change the lights. But you can change your attitude."

She's right. All anybody needs to change his or her entire life around, in fact, is the willingness to change attitudes.

The millennium hoopla is a perfect excuse for us to change our attitudes—about a lot of things. They say that the millennium is a cleansing time for the planet. Subconsciously, we think we're going to wake up on January 1st and have new lives. Our culture has suffered from a lot of bad habits long enough. It's ripe for recovery. Whether the recovery is from alcohol or drugs or food or shopping or gambling, I think people are finally willing to address some of their demons. You simply can't live with drug abuse or physical abuse or emotional abuse—and you can't live separate, without relationships. Those things *have* to be worked on. We need to mend the separatism and strive for unity in our relationships with one another and with God.

I think that God has created a wondrous mosaic. And in it, He has placed each one of us—we are all these little different colored stones. And every once in a while He lets us out of the mosaic to admire His work. He lets us see what He's created and where we are in it, and that's a privilege. I feel that in the rare times when I've been quiet and humble and willing to really look, He's shown it to me.

And then I go back into my place in the mosaic and do my thing, which is to shine for Him.

MUSIC APPRECIATION

I admit it—I didn't like The Beatles when they first came out. I didn't just resent their becoming more popular than the DJs. I really thought *She Loves You* was a horrible record. And I was forced to play *I Want to Hold Your Hand* too many times. Besides, I was into rhythm and blues, which is what I felt The Beatles were ripping off. I liked the original R&B artists. I used to go see James Brown, Otis Redding, and Chuck Berry—I didn't want to hear The Beatles doing their version of Chuck Berry. To me, they were like bad Chicago singers. We didn't need to have four guys from England with bad haircuts coming over here singing Little Richard songs.

But as I got older, I started to look beyond my resentment. And today, looking back, what astounds me is that The Beatles, who were probably abusing drugs and alcohol just as much as I was, wrote the most wonderful, spiritual songs—like *All You Need Is Love, Eleanor Rigby, Hey Jude,* and John Lennon's *Give Peace a Chance.* You could go through all of their records and you won't find "Paul is dead"—you'll find that God is alive.

CHAPTER 8

Comedy and Conscience

. . . And dance like nobody's watching.

I try not to confuse ratings with listeners. I don't owe my career to ratings; I owe it to listeners. I don't do my show for numbers on a page, for some scientifically chosen focus group that management assembled out in Piscataway. I do my show for flesh-and-blood folks who could be my friends and neighbors. I respect and appreciate my listeners not only because it's my job to, but also because listening is not a skill that I myself have thoroughly mastered. . . .

You'd think that, as a talk radio host, I'd know when to shut up and listen. But it hasn't always been so easy. In fact, people have screamed at me, yet I didn't hear a word they were saying. People have cried in my arms, and I still didn't listen. I'm learning now how important listening—really *listening*—is. It's something we all need to work at. It doesn't necessarily come naturally.

Here, for example, is a cautionary tale about what can happen when you don't listen to your wife.

When WNBC hired me away from Philadelphia oldies station WFIL in the mid-Eighties, I commuted from Philly to the Big Apple. But the manager of the station encouraged my wife and me to buy a house closer to New York—he gave us the impression I'd be at WNBC for a long time. So we went ahead and bought a house in New Jersey. It took us a while, but we moved all of our stuff and got settled. Then NBC was sold, and I was out.

My wife was pissed off at the station manager. She said, "He knew they were selling the station and yet he encouraged us to go ahead and buy a house here!"

Carolyn sat on the steps of the house in Jersey and cried. She said, "Why do we have to move again and everybody else in the neighborhood gets to stay?"

I said, "Well, because I'm in this business. Getting a new job means moving to a new city."

That was the rub. She said, "Well, you've got one more move left."

I was very careful in choosing my next job. I wanted to be in a place where Carolyn could put down roots and do the things she liked to do (golf, for one). A station in Connecticut offered me a morning show for around a quarter of a million dollars—and offered to buy me a house. But I turned it down. I thought the market was too risky and the climate was too cold for Carolyn. I decided to go to Florida where the weather was better for golf. I would've liked to have gone back to California, but I figured Carolyn had had enough of the show business scene.

So we got a beautiful home on a golf course in Florida. I took a radio job with an Italian guy—I figured I'd work for a paisano for a change. Up till then, I'd mostly worked for Jews. And in this case, I wished I still had—it was the worst mistake ever.

The WSHE owner made me the morning man. He said he'd give me a lot of freedom. I did a brief trial run to see whether I'd like it, and he gave me the freedom he promised. But after I took the job, little by little, he started to take my freedom away. He had something else in mind for the show, but he couldn't put it into words. This happens all the time—management really has something else in mind, but they don't tell you what it is. They just find a new guy.

That experience soured me on Florida. I wanted to move again. I needed to move again. Radio was my mistress—and she was breaking up my marriage.

Ten years have gone by now since Carolyn and I divorced. But I'm just starting to figure out what went wrong. The other night I thought I'd finally figured it out, and I asked Carolyn why she divorced me. "Was it because of NBC?" I asked. "We got divorced because of radio, right?"

"No," she said. "We got divorced because you wouldn't listen."

Now here's a tale about what can happen when you listen really well to your wife: It involves Tony Mamarella, who was my manager early in my career. A starmaker, he was also the producer of *American Bandstand*. In the early Sixties, he and his wife went to London and met The Beatles, whose first record released in America, *Please Please Me*, hadn't done particularly well. Tony listened to a few of their new songs, but wasn't that impressed.

His wife, however, was crazy about *She Loves You*. Though he didn't really like the song, he listened to his wife and bought her the American distribution rights to the record (for about $500), and released it in the States on his little record label, Swan.

The rest, as they say, is history.

LIVE WITH REGIS AND JOEY LEE!

*A*bout ten years ago, NBC sent some of its
celebrities, including me and Regis Philbin, out to
New Jersey to promote a new mall. I told jokes and
Regis sang Irish songs.

The next week Regis broadcast a show out in
front of the Apollo Theater, and I made a stupid,
off-color crack about it on my radio show. I never
forgot what I'd said, and ten years later when I was
on his show promoting my cheesecakes, I apologized. He barely remembered it, but he was a
stand-up guy for accepting my apology. Although
he did point out that if I was really sorry, I
would've apologized long before I had something I
wanted to promote on his show. . . .

Some people need managers, promoters, and other assorted starmakers in order to become celebrities. Others are just born stars.

Like one of my best friends, Rod Roddy, the regal announcer for *The Price Is Right*. He started out as disc jockey Hot Rod Roddy. I met him in Pittsburgh where he was the number one DJ the year the Pirates won the World Series. He was very clever, colorful, and successful. I helped him get a job in Buffalo, and we worked there together for a few years. The radio station had a basketball team, which he and I played on. Actually, I played and he emceed. Rod wouldn't play because, according to him, "Stars don't sweat."

Roddy eventually went to work at KLIF in Dallas. He had a radio talk show, and one night he insulted his guest, the reigning Miss America. (In his studio there was room enough for only one person to wear a crown, and it wasn't going to be her.) Whatever he said, she responded by throwing coffee on him. So he feigned a heart attack. They took him to Parkland Memorial (the same hospital where they took President Kennedy after his assassination), and within the hour he was set up in his own private room and was ordering a special meal from the menu.

A few years back, Roddy and I met in Buffalo for our old radio station's 25th reunion. Since he considered himself a CBS TV star, he demanded a limo, a first-class room, and a first-class flight. He even brought his own shower nozzle because he liked a certain kind of spray on his tushy. But on his way back to L.A., he forgot to pack the shower nozzle in the luggage he checked, so he had to put it in a carry-on bag.

The flight crew, however, wouldn't let him take the nozzle on board—the pipe was classified as a weapon or something. He bickered back and forth with the airline people. Furious, he finally had to leave it behind and let them mail it to him. A disgruntled passenger who was irritated by the delay that Roddy's skirmish was causing yelled that Roddy could take the nozzle and shove it up his ass. Roddy replied, "Well, *what do you think it's for?*"

Do you ever wonder where they get ideas for movies and comedy shows today? Do you know where the heart of comedy comes from? AA meetings. All these writers are in AA, listening to other people's stories of decline and devastation. I swear, I go to movies today and think, "Hey, wait a second . . . that looks familiar. . . ."

It's ironic, but a lot of great comedy comes out of pain, whether it's the pain of addiction or of loneliness or of disease or of misfortune. Do you ever wonder why some of our best comedians have had such screwed-up lives? That's why they're great comedians—they're mining their own material and trying to make some real heavy shit feel light. If everything is going along great for you, you're already smiling and don't need to think up a great comedy. It's often the folks who are in the most pain who come up with the best laughs—as a way to combat the pain.

Comedy is the silver lining to life's misfortunes. But we have to be willing to laugh at ourselves to fully benefit from our hardships.

I think some perfectly sober writers go to AA just to write. Like "Baker's Secret," it's Writer's Secret—go to AA meetings, get everybody's material, and pretend you thought it up first.

FOOD FOR THOUGHT

I lost one of my best friends last year. Tom Shovan, who had owned *Pulse* magazine and syndicated programs on radio stations across the country, passed away. The radio business will miss him dearly. He was a forward-thinking man—when he was driving out of Dallas on his way to New York, he'd be counting out exact change for the Jersey tollbooth.

Tom was a huge influence on me. Tom was huge, period. I've never met a man with an appetite like his. I remember once we were out in Providence, Rhode Island, at a joint on the beach called Custy's that offered an all-you-could-eat lobster meal for $18.00. So Tom, some friends, and I set up camp there around noon. We brought cards. We played through dinner. By that time, of course, I never wanted to see another lobster. But Tom had eaten 63! That's 63 lobsters in one (albeit day-long) sitting. It made the front page of the *Providence Journal*. When asked how he could've eaten that many lobsters, he replied, "On a lobster, you know, there's not a lot of meat."

Have you ever found that something you once rebelled against is what you end up embracing with greater understanding later?

Remember in the beginning of the book when I told you how I ran far and fast away from the priests at Bishop Timon High School? Well, I eventually returned to the church. I think we inherit some religious ideas from our parents, test the waters on our own, and then revisit religion if we can.

I guess you could call me a "born again" Christian, but I'm suspicious of the label. I think that's what certain self-righteous people who've been devout all their lives call newcomers to the church in order to separate themselves and make themselves feel superior.

Remember the story of the prodigal son? The prodigal son runs away from his family, squanders his money on wine and women, and basically does everything wrong (that's me). Even though he's made a terrible mess of things, his father (that's God) receives him back, throws him a big shindig, and restores his place in the family. A lot of people think that's where the story ends, that the story is just about God's forgiveness.

But the story is also about the other son. When the father threw a big party for the prodigal son, it really angered the "good" son, who had been loyal to his father all along and never made all those terrible mistakes. He got jealous. He thought, "Why is Dad making such a fuss over *him*—he should be rewarding me for being so good and loyal!" So the other son was not as virtuous as he thought he was—he was guilty of the sin of jealousy. He didn't understand why the father would pay such attention to his brother.

Well, the jealous son represents the church. Often, people who've been faithful all their lives and have never strayed tend to look down on us "prodigal" Christians. So the sin in the story is not just the philandering of the prodigal son. The sin lies with the other son, too, because it's a sin to think that you're better than someone else just because you've remained faithful.

Bouncing from radio station to radio station, drug to drug, and bad attitude to worse attitude has made me pretty appreciative of the friends, fans, and fellow Christians (not to mention God) who have stuck with me over the years.

I say, let's welcome back as many screwed-up prodigals as we can find . . . I mean, did somebody say *party*??